Scrapbook of an Unfound Songstress

by
Vicky Nolan

ISBN-13: 978-1979124904
ISBN-10: 1979124906

Design & formatting by Socciones Editoria Digitale
www.kindle-publishing-service.co.uk

Contents

A Little Note ii

1. Any ideas? What's the story? 1

2. Hearing the beat, finding my rhythm 20

3. The Introduction 44

4. Noodling my lyrics - eh? 52

5. Oath and first verse 68

6. Canyons and melodies 78

7. Give me the chorus baby! 91

8. Stay composed, and just ad lib 101

9. Brooklyn… is that the bridge? 116

10. A mad tea party 125

11. It's all in the producer's mix 134

12. The final cut 149

13. Call the publisher 162

14. Sorry... Was I out of Key? 167

15. A public performance 173

The Outro 182

A Little Note

Picturesque Norcliffe Chapel, Styal, Cheshire. – built in 1823 in the gothic revival style – nestles comfortably in the English countryside. A pitched roof of Kerridge stone and slate; lancet windows and a three-bay chancel; wild honeysuckle and clematis climbing the red brick walls, reaching for the rose window at its top apex. The warm summer sunshine bathes the scene; how pretty the church looks.

The open gabled porch stands before you, its oak timber frame welcoming you inside. Within the chapel sit the guests, a happy sense of occasion in the air. The smell of candles and spent wicks float through the church, scented white roses embellish the pews. Everything's ready.

Without cue, there falls a respectful hush, the silence broken only by the sound of whispered chatter and the clearing of people's throats. The wedding ceremony is about to begin.

The minister stands at the lectern and addresses the congregation: "Friends, there are a variety of ways we can express joy, and we first do so in song, offered to us today by Victoria."

A young child of a girl, with plaited baby's breath hair, makes herself known and politely moves out from the pew. She quietly walks down the aisle towards the altar, leaving only the sound of faint footsteps behind her.

She steps onto the stage, holds the mic, and looks up to face the audience. She waits... Silence falls across the chapel as she pauses.

The grand pipe organ starts and then the notes on the pedal keyboard are played: Chords *G major, D and B... Melody A, C and E...*

The girl smiles, opens her mouth, and sings.

"We've only just begun…"

1

Any Ideas? What's the story?

There I was, sitting with my dad in the back seat of a taxi, heading for Manchester Airport. We were on our way to Copenhagen, which was exciting enough, but the most exciting thing was that we were going courtesy of Polydor Records, something which gave me the chills just thinking about it. Apparently, they had 'seen something' in me and were paying for a few days' of recording and songwriting sessions in the Danish capital. At first, I thought it was a joke, and now it was actually happening, I still couldn't quite believe it.

I was just a fresh-faced, gawky fifteen-year-old, working the odd weekend as a pot-washer for cash and still doing my GCSE's at school. Well, not today. While my friends were slaving away at their desks, counting the minutes until home-time, I was jetting off to try my hand at being a pop star for a few days. It's all I've ever wanted to be. When I was 11 years old I played Alice in my school's production of Alice in Wonderland and not for one moment did I ever imagine that just four years later I'd be recording with producers and songwriters that I looked up to. Dreams really can come true.

Of course, because of my age, Mum had insisted on Dad going with me and being my chaperone. Wishful thinking would have liked me to have gone on my own, but in reality, I wasn't really ready or mature enough to look after myself just yet – as much as I hated to admit it, I needed him there; I was still a teenager adjusting to living in a world full of grown-ups, and this trip was bound to be eye-opening in that regard. Well, a girl can't have everything, can she? At least not right away; good things come to those who wait, and I could wait.

Breathless with excitement, I stared out of the window as we approached the airport, the butterflies in my stomach getting bigger with every mile. In my head, I pretended I was on one of those MTV Diary specials; I imagined being like Britney Spears – globetrotting, performing sold out shows and recording platinum albums, all the while looking incredibly beautiful and glamorous. If only.

Dad was glancing at his watch – clearly worried we might miss the flight – and his voice brought me out of my nice daydream. "This is your big break, Vicky," he said, smiling. "If you can pull it off, the world's your oyster! Carpe Diem... Carpe Diem!"

I couldn't help but laugh – it was typical Dad; a born optimist, he was always telling me to seize the day. Carpe Diem, Carpe Diem, over and over again. Well, I guessed it had worked, because here I was.

Taking a deep breath, I tried to keep calm but I just couldn't. The pressure was building, my dad's nervous energy infectious. I pretended that I was taking it all in my stride, but inside I was quaking from giddiness and nerves in equal measure.

Finally, the taxi dropped us off outside Departures and we hurried inside with our luggage. It was crowded, with throngs of people on the go everywhere you looked, the atmosphere full of a buzz and expectation.

Waiting for us was my manager William Robinson; he spotted us through the crowds and shouted over, "Hey Kevin, Vicky!" before striding over to us. "Hi, my little superstar! How are you?" He beamed at me, making me blush.

I was blushing because – as usual – people were staring at us; William sure loved to make a scene, alright. He'd been my manager and promoter for about six months and it was fair to say that he exuded a jolly optimism with the volume turned up to the max. I knew then though that he had my best interests at heart, but little did I know how much trouble he'd go on to cause me.

Dressed from top to toe in the best black suit he owned, William was a chubby northerner in his mid-thirties who bore an uncanny resemblance to Peter Kay the comedian. He even sounded a bit like him, hence my slight embarrassment at his loud greeting. "Great to see you, all set?" he asked with a wide grin, as he put his arm around my skinny shoulders.

As usual, lying across his right shoulder was his trendy canvas bag, emblazoned with the Midem music industry logo. I guessed it was his way of saying, 'Yeah, that's right, look at us: we're in the music business'. Despite the Peter Kay thing he had going on, he always tried to look his best, and he always played the part and was professional – unlike Dad, who favoured the more dishevelled look: unshaven, unkempt hair and wearing his best checked lumberjack shirt for the occasion. Perhaps he was trying to be 'cool'. As much as I loved him, he also got on my nerves. You could say, I was a typical teenager in this regard. He was naturally down-to-earth and he'd talk to anyone that would listen to him – that was the blarney in him – his Irish blarney. I found it odd that he wore his prescription sunglasses indoors. I suppose he was being practical as he couldn't be bothered to carry around two pairs with him. Maybe he thought that made him look cool too? I wasn't quite so convinced.

We boarded the Scandinavian Airlines flight around 10:30 a.m., and as we prepared for take-off, William and Dad talked endlessly about their plans for the future. *My* future. Recording contracts, world tours, Grammys… you name it, they had it all figured out. They were expecting big things from me. Huge things.

I, however, found this all a little too far-fetched, despite my daydreams of world stardom. The last time I looked in the mirror I was still a gangly teenager who hadn't fully grown into herself yet; could I really fit into the world of glitzy showbiz? Could I really share the world stage with all of my idols? A world where the girls were all body-confident, glossy and flawless? I didn't even know who I was yet, who I was going to turn out to be. How could I take on such a responsibility if I didn't know who I was?

I was scared that if I dared to believe all this could be possible, I would fall into a pit of disappointment and regret – and all before I turned sweet sixteen.

I turned to my two chaperones, listening to them talk about me like I wasn't there – the more excited they became, the louder they spoke, and the more attention they were getting from the other passengers. I could see people staring over at us, wondering who this little girl was who was being talked about in such an amazing way.

I squirmed in my seat, knowing what they must have been thinking. While I was fifteen, I looked about twelve: blonde, slightly built, and with an air of innocence that bordered on the naive.

Yes, naive is what I was: I had no idea of what lay ahead. It was a good job, really; if I'd have known then what I know now, I'd have unbuckled my seatbelt right there and run all the way back home to Poynton. Too late now.

Just then, the aircraft taxied to a halt and swung round for take-off, making my stomach churn a little. All this talk of fame had put my nerves on edge, and I was now even more unsettled than before. I hid my anxiety behind a mask of teenage cool, slipping on my headphones that started to blare Beyoncé's *Crazy in Love* through my ears. That was just how that moment felt: a little crazy.

As the engines roared and we thundered down the runway, my stomach churned again. I've often read that famous people describe the first moments of fame as being exactly like that – like an aircraft taking off – but I hadn't realised how scary it would be.

Moments later, we had taken off and were heading into the unknown, in more ways than one.

During the flight, I kept glancing over at William, who was talking nonstop to my Dad about the music business. I knew that William had gone into a business association with Robin Gibb and his manager Ken Graydon, both of whom were supporting me and helping me develop my career.

Needless to say, I was very flattered that such a high-profile artist such as Robin Gibb liked me and was actually interested in my project. I'd always admired the Bee Gees (though I was young, I'd grown up on this kind of music thanks to my Mum and Dads disco dancing), appreciating that they wrote incredible songs, and the song *Immortality* was one of my favourites: *"So this is who I am!"*

So how exactly had this trip come about? Well, Ken (Robin's Manager) had sent some of my demos over to Robin's record label – Polydor – and they liked them. Next thing I knew, I was rushing down the M6 to London to meet the top man at Polydor, Colin Barlow. It was as quick as that.

I can remember walking into Polydor's reception at Black Lion Lane and just thinking, *wow!* So, this is where it all happens!

Ken greeted us and then took us into Colin's office for the meeting, a room fitting for a big music executive: his walls were covered in gold records and decked out in expensive hi-fi equipment and CD's – no expense spared. Dad had made a joke about the Liverpool football scarf lying on the desk (Dad being a dyed-in-the-wool Man U fan), and everyone laughed. As it turned out, Colin was a really nice guy; he was young and understated, and the total opposite of how you'd imagine a big music exec to be – the anti-Simon Cowell, if you will. He could see that I was nervous but he made me feel at ease as we chatted about my musical interests and the direction I wanted to take.

After a few more minutes of talking, and to my amazement, he casually said to me, "Right Vicky, I'm sending you to Copenhagen and booking you in with a Danish production and songwriting team called Deekay Music." I was gobsmacked, and though I didn't know it then, I later found out that Deekay Music were made up of producers who had worked with the likes of Ronan Keating, Samantha Mumba, the Sugababes and Blue.

It all seemed so simple: I was going to Copenhagen, just like that. I couldn't believe it, and neither could any of my friends at school, when I told them. They thought I was either having them on, or that I'd gone mad. I'd already had to pinch myself to make sure it was true – things like that just didn't happen to an everyday school girl, do they? – and when my friends initially doubted me,

I thought I must be dreaming.

But here it was… actually happening! Now I *knew* I wasn't dreaming.

An hour and a half later, we landed in Copenhagen before grabbing a taxi into the city. It was early spring, and the whole place was covered in melting slush and snow – apart from the roads, which had been swept and were now clear, unlike in England, where everything seems to grind to a shuddering halt when there's even the lightest of snowfalls. No, here the roads were full of buses and bicycles all on the move, the weather slowing no one down. The city moved casually on, and soon I'd be a part of it.

When we drove across a flyover, I got my first proper view of Copenhagen, a historic city of canals, cobbled squares, and copper spires. Its picturesque buildings and famous harbour were all nestled beneath a shimmering dusting of white snow, giving it a Christmas chocolate box feel about it.

We carried on through the beautiful city and soon we were at our hotel, the Radisson Blue Scandinavian, which was an impressive twenty-six-storey steel and glass skyscraper. Situated on the outskirts of the city centre, it was designed by a guy called Arne Jacobson, apparently one of Denmark's best architects. See? I may not have been at school, but I was still learning things.

We got out of the taxi and took our luggage inside, out of the cold. I looked around us, smiling. The foyer housed a number of designer shops, which immediately made me plan for my first activity: window-shopping. I could pretend to be just like Julia Roberts in Pretty Woman, just without the credit cards, the sugar daddy, or the thigh-high PVC boots.

I was in my element, but my good mood soon dissolved when Dad told me that we were to share a twin room. Loud snoring wasn't really the recipe for a great night's sleep when a girl needed to look and sing like a superstar!

I'll admit, I was more than a little ticked-off at the news; this was a nerve-wracking trip, and I wanted to have my own space, carry my own room key, watch what I wanted on TV. I was a little miffed. But even though my Dad got on my nerves, I secretly enjoyed sharing the experience with him, plus I knew he liked any excuse to get away from the humdrum of regular life. So, I'd just have to put up with his snoring for a few nights. And I guess he'd have to put up my snoring as well. (Yes, I snore).

We all settled into our rooms, and in the evening, all three of us made our way to the ground floor to have dinner in the hotel's swanky a la carte restaurant. The menu had all sorts of posh things on offer: *lobster, salad and cress with strips of Parma ham; roast duck with morels, beetroot and long peppers; and chocolate, hazelnut and spices*. I'd never eaten in a place like this before – I couldn't pronounce half of the things on the menu, but it definitely beat the fish and chips from the Strawberry Pig Chippy in my local village. Yes, I thought I could get used to this type of fine dining, even If I did get a little confused by the puzzling number of knives and forks on the table. In the end, I gave up trying to guess which one to use and just used all of them. It seemed easier.

During dinner, William and Dad hatched a plan to visit the hotel casino later that evening.

"Am I invited?" I asked jokingly. I didn't *really* want to go, though it would have been pretty cool.

Dad laughed. "Sorry, Vicky, you're far too young – your mum would kill me if she knew you'd been into a casino!"

William nodded in agreement, though his mind was more on the studio session. "Your Dad's right. Anyway, you'll be singing tomorrow for the Deekay guys. I want your voice nice and rested superstar"

I agreed, secretly happy that I'd have the room to myself, and several minutes later, I was lying on my bed, flicking through the TV channels. I tried not to think about the next day, about the nerves that were currently building up inside me – I was worried that if I thought about it too much, I wouldn't want to do it.

So instead, I sat back and relaxed.

The next morning after breakfast – which was Danish, of

course (had to get that in!) we made our way to the foyer for our ten o'clock meet and greet with the guys from Deekay Music.

By now I was more than a little bit tense – these guys were the real-deal, professional producers after all - but Dad helped me calm down with a pep talk. He loved pep talks. "Just be yourself, Vicky. You'll be fine. Carpe Diem.... Seize the day!"

Well, that was easy for him to say; he didn't have to write the songs or do any of the singing!

Suddenly, the revolving entrance doors to the hotel whirled like a prism, and in stepped three good-looking guys in their late twenties. I could tell straight away that they were record producers; they had that unmistakable confident swagger that comes from loving what you do.

One of the guys, the tallest, scanned the foyer and marched straight over to where we were sitting. He looked at me in a knowing way and said, "Hi Vicky, so this is the artist!"

I jumped to my feet with a big smile, hoping my enthusiasm would cover up my nerves. "Yeah, that's me!"

"Hi, my name's Lars Jensen. This is my co-producer, Martin Larsson, and one of our songwriters, Obi. It's great to be working with you, Vicky. We've heard a lot about you."

All three gave me a hug, which surprised me. They were so friendly and approachable; there was no sign of self-importance or ego whatsoever. They were also polite and extremely professional, which immediately made me relax, my nerves vanishing.

"Right," said Lars. "Let's go to the studio. We'll walk if you don't mind; it's only a few blocks from here, and we can chat and get to know one another on the way."

All six of us agreed and we left the Radisson, strolling out into the chilly morning air. Another light dusting of snow had covered the ground overnight and everywhere we went looked so picturesque – just like a postcard you'd buy from a quaint little memento shop. We walked along the spacious streets and boulevards, passing apartment blocks, bikes, chic cafes, bikes, delicatessens, bikes… you get the picture!

Bicycles filled the streets everywhere – it was true what people said about the Danes: they were mad about cycling. The other thing I noticed was that most of the bikes left outside their apartments and shops didn't have locks on them; Copenhagen must be a very trusting city.

We turned left, heading up Njalsgade, and halfway along the street we came to a six-storey building. The first two storeys were built from light-coloured stone blocks with elegant arched windows, while the upper floors were made of a more mundane red brick.

Lars took us inside, leading us up to the top floor by way of an old elevator, which creaked and whined when coming to a stop. The noise added to my sense of expectation, the nerves trickling their way back in now that we were actually here. Opening the lift doors with some force, we stepped into the loft space where Deekay had their offices and recording studios. They had two studios in all, and they were both very impressive.

Pushing open the door, I was immediately struck by the calming ambience created by the cool Scandinavian decor – beech floorboards stripped and laminated, offset by walls and ceilings painted in neutral greys and whites. The modernist theme continued with the lighting; I stared up at the stainless-steel tracks with lights that were suspended from the ceiling. Incorporated into the studio was a small, minimalist kitchen decorated in bold colours and furnished in the Pop Art, avant-garde style of the 60's. It all seemed very Ikea inspired, and I loved it.

Next door to the kitchen was a chill-out room where artists could write and relax. The corridors were adorned with pop music memorabilia, and there were random splashes of gold and platinum-coloured disks hung to the walls, celebrating their chart successes.

Inside the control room was a 64-track digital mixing desk facing a tinted glass screen behind which lay a large soundproofed room, again full of rock and roll paraphernalia – a drum kit surrounded by a whole host of guitars and keyboards.

A glass-fronted sound booth stood in one corner, kitted out with a single microphone and bunches of headphones. This for me, it was the crucible, the epicentre of creativity, and I couldn't wait to get in there and start creating.

There were big leather chairs in front of the mixing desk that looked like something out of the Starship Enterprise, as well as acres and acres of sliders and flat screen monitors, all powered by Pro Tools software and Apple Mac computers. They had all of the plugins at their fingertips, it was mind blowing. I'd recorded in a few studios in the Stockport and Manchester areas before, but they were second-rate and amateurish in comparison to this. It was a bit like comparing a new Ferrari to a second-hand Ford Focus.

This place was on a whole different level I'd always had a vision of recording somewhere like this, but I never really thought I'd get the chance or opportunity to do it. Everything was so cutting edge, and I felt right at home. I couldn't wait to get going. Let me in!

"OK," said Lars. "Let's get to work."

Dad and William said their goodbyes, then William passed on Robin Gibb's and Ken Graydon's best wishes for the session to the Deekay team, and then Lars led me into the studio.

Even though I thought I had my nerves under control, as soon as we entered the room, a swarm of butterflies took flight in my stomach. I didn't show it, though; I didn't want them thinking I couldn't handle this.

I took a deep breath, trying to calm down. There was nowhere to hide now; it was time to believe and trust in my talent. I just hoped I'd be good enough.

To start with, there was just talk, and a lot of it; Lars and I chatted for hours, as he wanted to get a sense of who I was and what I wanted to sing about. Then we started throwing ideas around, working on melodies, lyrics, and stories that we wanted to share in the songs. Whilst we did this, the others were putting together the production. It was a slick operation, a digital record factory!

Over the next few hours, we batted our ideas around between the five of us, making it a truly collaborative effort. I spent a few hours with Lars and Martin, and then Obi and Jay, and soon the basic structure of the songs had begun to take shape. It was such a joy to be working with such talented people; I was truly inspired, and for the first time, I felt really good about the lyrics I was writing. These weren't just scribbles I made in my notebook whilst watching Nickelodeon; these were real thoughts and emotions. Poetry, really – I was writing musical poetry!

It's time for the girls to rally to the front
And give the people at the party what they want
I got my squad and we're coming through
And don't it make it cool seem to you
And we take off in a moment, strap your seatbelt

After a while, Lars went back into the control room to lay down the backing track with Martin – this involved drums, guitar, bass, and keyboard, including all of the audio tricks. It was so exciting to hear it start to take shape, and I began to wonder what other people would think when they heard it too – my friends, my family, people from back home. It was all a bit surreal.

After lunch, Dad and William returned to watch and hear me lay down the vocals, and while it was nice to have them there, everyone peering through the glass in the control room did make me feel like I was in a fish bowl. Disregarding the stares, I shut myself in and slid on a pair of headphones, speaking as confidently as I could into the state-of-the-art microphone. "One two, one two, check." I smiled, thinking, 'that's what they say, don't they?'

Lars's voice came into my ear, "OK, Vicky. Let's go for a take."

The next second, the intro to the song started washing through the headphones, and with my heart pounding, I scanned my hastily scribbled lyrics, closed my eyes, and began to sing the opening bars of the song. I just let all of my fears and worries go, and focused on the words. My words. Dad told me later that when I started to sing, Lars had smiled at Martin and said, "Well, she's got perfect pitch and tone." Which was a huge compliment.

When I'd finished the first run-through, both Lars and Martin grinned from behind the glass screen and gave me the big thumbs up, causing a wave of relief to roll over me. I was overjoyed, but I kept telling myself: composure, composure, composure. I needed to look professional, like I was taking it all in my stride.

We worked on the backing vocals for a while and then I went back into the control room to listen to and appraise the track. I couldn't believe the quality of the production and how good my voice sounded. It sounded like a real record, like one you'd hear on the radio and sing along to!

This was it. Things were starting to happen.

The next few days were dedicated to songwriting and recording, as well as exploring new ideas. Part of the time I'd write with Lars and Martin – who were slick pop maestros, noted for being current and finding the right sound for their artists – and the rest of the time I'd work with Obi and Jay, two young, up-and-coming producers who preferred a more laid-back, collaborative style.

We soon fell into a typical studio regime of starting late and finishing late, from late morning to gone eleven at night – and sometimes even longer – with the odd break for a sandwich and a cup of tea. There was a lot of tea.

As I got more comfortable, I started making silly jokes and quoting lines from movies I loved, like *Dumb and Dumber*. They laughed, telling me I was funny, which made me relax more than anything else did – I was having a great time! My confidence was soaring with each day that passed, and I made a real effort to look my best – making a good impression was vital in this business, and I was starting to learn exactly how to do that. Combat-style army pants were big at the time, and I teamed them with a tight pink cotton top and baby blue Timberland boots. I looked the part, and I was starting to feel like I really belonged there. It was the first time I actually felt like I was growing into myself, going from a young woman into the part of a serious singer songwriter. It felt good.

During our writing sessions, Lars and Martin really pushed me vocally, experimenting with challenging harmonies and intricate vocal lines. It was incredibly fun and it was so exhilarating hearing what my voice could do, especially as everything sounded so polished and professional. I'd done a lot of demos in the past but nothing like this – nothing that sounded so promising, so real. For a few moments, I actually started to believe I could be a pop star, that I could live this life and be successful. Suddenly, I wasn't that timid teenager who had boarded the plane in England. I was becoming who I was meant to be.

One morning, I had a bit of spare time before going to the studio so Dad took me sightseeing around Copenhagen. The weather was stunning, my idea of the perfect day – bright blue sky with a touch of frost – and it made the beautiful city seem even more amazing.

We decided to wrap up warm and walk into the city centre – dodging the bikes as we went – the route taking us through the famous Tivoli Gardens, a fairy-tale amusement park with old-fashioned rides, romantic pagodas and bandstands, and beautifully laid out flower beds. It was like stepping back into the late 18th Century and going for a hushed walk with Hans Christian Anderson *"Where words fail, music speaks,"* It was a resting break from the crazy few days I'd been having – it gave me time to breathe, to take everything in.

We strolled around the harbour with its iconic mermaid statue as the fresh sea breeze bit at our faces. The densely packed medieval streets – with names that were impossible to pronounce – were filled with tourists and locals eating at the road-side cafes and restaurants, and it struck me how family-oriented the Danes were, and how effortlessly relaxed everyone seemed to be. It was a gentle cultured place, and I was starting to feel quite worldly myself, like I'd broken out of my little bubble and was starting to see what else was out there, what else I could experience in life. For the first time, I felt really grown up, more mature.

Dad took me for lunch in a cafe situated on a cobbled square, and we dined al fresco like the locals, taking it all in. To think that my friends were all at school was more than a little strange, and I almost had to pinch myself again to make sure it was all real.

By now the studio was calling me, so I only had time to window shop, but that was fine with me: I gazed dreamily into the glitzy boutiques, mentally spending money I didn't have. Yet. One day, I promised myself, I'd be able to treat myself, as well as my family.

Over a three-day period, we wrote and recorded four soulful Pop/R'n'B songs: *As If*, *Hate Myself for Loving You*, *Boy Is Not A Man* and *What You Want*. I'll never forget those song titles; they were the start of everything, and they'll always be a part of me.

Lars and Martin surprised me by bringing in a couple of local rappers, adding a splash of street cred to the tracks that I alone wouldn't have been able to achieve. I was blown away at how bloody cool they made me sound! We all agreed on copyright ownership for the songs – which was all new to me – and then we were done.

It was a wonderful experience, and it was difficult to leave all the fun and excitement behind so I could return back to school in the UK, but on the fourth day I had to do just that.

After checking out of the hotel – and before Dad could query the bill – we popped back to the studio to say our goodbyes to Lars, Martin, Obi and the rest of the production team. I'll never forget that special time I spent with them. They were the kindest group of guys you could ever wish to be with and work with, fizzing with enthusiasm and creativity and making me feel like an equal member of the team. They clearly loved their jobs, and they'd made me love it too. They'd made me feel like I was worthy of this kind of experience, rather than the imposter I'd felt like on the plane. I felt sad about leaving, but I couldn't wait for it all to happen again.

On the flight home we were all elated, in high spirits – why wouldn't we be? William was convinced that the songs were strong and would impress Colin Barlow at Polydor, and he was hopeful that they would clinch a record deal with a major, but only time would tell.

I never liked to count my chickens before they've hatched – and I still don't – so I wasn't getting too carried away. I was cautious, but optimistically cautious. It was hard not to be.

Staring out of the aircraft, I gazed at the passing clouds, deep in thought. Looking through the window...

Every day the world keeps turning,

so don't let it pass on by,

you can have what your heart is yearning,

got to climb on for the ride

As the plane touched down in Manchester, a party of school children on the plane burst into spontaneous applause, cheering and clapping loudly as they celebrated the pilot's successful landing.

It was strange, but their noisy exuberance seemed to sum up my time in Copenhagen: crazy and full of happiness.

A success. A job well done.

I just hoped Polydor Records would feel the same.

FADE IN :

INT. GRYPHONS SOLICITORS. MR LORY'S OFFICE.
MANCHESTER. DAY.

MR LORY a junior lawyer in his mid-twenties,
rises as VICKY enters the office.

                    MR LORY
     Hello Vicky, nice to see you again.

They shake hands. He motions to a chair.

                    MR LORY
          Please, take a seat.

VICKY sits.

                    MR LORY
          Now, where are my notes.

MR LORY looks through a pile of papers on
his desk. VICKY stares at him anxiously.

                    MR LORY
Ah, here we are.......Right......You see,
Vicky, it's like this; it's all about your
music contracts, and the aspects around
contracts of necessity...... testing if
they're enforceable or not. As I've said,

It looks like this... they want to sue you
in court strictly on the issue of liability
in the first instance, and then, if they
win, the supposition is, the second trial
will investigate the issues around quantum.

VICKY looks confused.

MR LORY

Quantum merit, that is.

VICKY

What does that mean, Mr Lory? (quietly)

MR LORY

(leans forward in his chair)
Well, if they win on both counts you'll
probably be ruined financially... but don't
worry, that won't happen, they won't win.
(faint laughter)

SILENCE. VICKY looking shocked and
uncomfortable.

MR LORY

Any questions?

PAUSE

                    VICKY

Will...... will I have time to finish my
school exams Mr Lory?

SILENCE. MR LORY a blank expression.

Glimpses of Me… _Blurred Lines_

My bleary eyes blink. They blink again. They struggle to focus in the dark as the sun's minimal light struggles to seep through my bedroom curtains. Imagine a permanent oil painting, awash with a swish of colours but you can't really make out an image.

This is how I wake every day. My vision blurred by default. You could say that I'm visually impaired, specky-four-eyes, geek. My eyes started going bad from the age of 11. I noticed that I was struggling to read the writing on the board at school. "Oh no, maybe I need glasses?" I told my parents. My parents told me that I was fine and that if I got glasses it would probably make them worse. Looking back, I think they thought I was making it up. Maybe they thought I wanted to be like my favourite Spice Girl, Mel B when she occasionally wore glasses. After all, I had begged them for leopard print platforms for months on end because of her influence.

I begged my science teacher at high school to write in my planner to say that I had to sit at the front of the class to see at least something on the board. And he knew that I didn't even like science so he probably thought her eyes must be bad. It was enough to convince my parents, so we ventured to Specsavers for a gold-rimmed pair of Lennon-styled beauties and the rest is history. Let's just say I'm pretty sure Harry Potter modelled himself on my look, but of course I can't be certain.

2

Hearing the beat, finding my rhythm

"Right, Vicky, let's run through the scales one more time… and remember: chin up, shoulders back. Don't forget to breathe through your diaphragm."

"Yes, Mrs Nield."

It was Saturday morning and I was standing next to the piano in my music teacher's study, having one of my regular singing and music lessons. I was nine years old, taking the first tentative steps towards a career in music – although I didn't know it then, of course. At the time, I just sang for the love of it, for the sheer joy it brought me. That was all that mattered back then, and it's something I've never quite lost, despite everything that's happened since.

I still love music – that's something that never leaves you.

In fact, I was obsessed with music from a very early age – pretty much as soon as I could talk, I'd be singing and ad-libbing constantly, imitating my favourite singers of the time: Toni Braxton, Eternal, Anita Baker, and Lauryn Hill to name a few. I would rehearse song lyrics until I knew them word for word, and one of my favourite things was to stay up and watch pre-recorded performances on *Top of the Pops*, tirelessly practising the dance routines in front of the TV. I loved *Top of the Pops*, but when it came to magazines, my heart was with *Smash Hits* – that was my pop bible, and I never missed an issue.

I'd been driving my family potty with impromptu concerts for as long as I could remember… in the lounge, on the patio, on the driveway, pretty much anywhere I could get away with it. And it wasn't just for my family, either; if the neighbours were out the back and near our garden, I saw that as a chance to put on an even bigger show than usual.

Basically, I loved having an audience – my three sisters, my Mum and Dad, my grandparents – anyone who was hanging around had no choice but to listen. To put it simply, I was a pain!

I would wear my Mum's high heels, put on the biggest pair of clip-on earrings I could find in her jewellery box, and smear some of her bright red lipstick on my lips (and inevitably, my teeth). Then – and only then – would I be ready to belt out a tune. I was a bundle of kinetic energy; constantly moving, twitching, singing, dancing, and talking. I never stopped!

I believed that I could be anyone I wanted to be. I was a dreamer, and I knew how to dream big.

So you want to be a beauty queen, fly a plane or sell ice cream,

a dancer, a painter, an actor in a play, well… it's OK to dream.

But after all, everybody wants to find a happy place,

everybody wants to see a smiling face… Don't we all?

One day at school assembly, some of the kids from the year above gave a talk about how they were learning different kinds of musical instruments – flutes, clarinets, and violins – before giving a demonstration of their abilities. My interest immediately piqued, I looked at the violin and thought, 'I could do that!', just like you do when you're a precocious eight-year-old.

When I got home, I immediately started begging my Mum to buy me a violin and to send me for lessons. This came as a bit of a surprise, to say the least – no one in the family was even remotely musical, so my Mum was a little puzzled that I'd taken an interest. Still, she wanted to encourage me, but after considering it, she told me that it was too expensive.

Some kids would have dropped the subject after that, but not me; after a lot of nagging and persuasion – as well as promises that I'd be good – she finally relented and bought me a guitar. The main reason for getting a guitar instead of a violin was the cost – it was much cheaper, something my Dad liked the sound of. My parents were always a bit pushed for money when I was growing up, but who could blame them with four young daughters to look after? Yes, the cost of the guitar was good, but I have a sneaking suspicion that Mum also bought it me because she thought it would keep me occupied, making life a little easier for her.

After a few months of struggling to play *Greensleeves,* I discovered that my guitar teacher also taught singing. Before that, I didn't know there was such a thing – I just assumed singers had to figure it out for themselves. It was a revelation, and as soon as I found out, I couldn't wait to start being trained to sing.

I wanted to sing all the catchy pop songs I heard on the radio – Kylie Minogue, Whitney Houston, and Mariah Carey. That type of thing, however, it cut no ice with my music teacher; she insisted that I start from scratch, and that meant training my voice the professional way. There were no cutting corners as far as Mrs Nield was concerned.

So, I knuckled down to the arduous task of classical voice training, learning how to sight-read and reeling off the traditional, "Do-re-mi-fa-so-la-ti-do", like I was a child star in a musical.

Now, as I've mentioned, I loved singing, but the problem was that as a young student, I found this kind of thing – the whole process of classical voice training – quite dull and boring. What's a do-re-mi when you wanted to belt out your favourite pop songs? I would get told off and chastised for not applying myself to music theory properly, and for only relying on my vocal skill and performance. It happened over and over again.

Mrs Nield was a gifted musician who taught guitar, piano, and singing. A trained soprano with a loud, crystal clear voice, she was a rather large, formidable lady in her late forties with dark red shoulder length hair teased into loose, frizzy curls. She had a keen eye for matching colours, embellishing her outfits with her favourite knitted ponchos or cardigans emblazoned with groovy

70's-style prints. She also wore massive circular glasses that gave her face a 'wise owl' kind of appearance. Her wrists were adorned with bangles and bracelets that matched her jewelled earrings, and when she moved she would often sound like a wind chime. Let's just say that she made a big impression on everyone she met, and I was no exception.

She taught her lessons from her home, a semi-detached bungalow in Bramhall (a leafy suburb near Stockport, Greater Manchester), which she shared with her quiet husband Ken and a large brood of cats. She was an exceptional lady, and a true inspiration for many people. Born with spina bifida and confined to a wheelchair, she never complained about anything, instead always putting others first.

Her energy was boundless – which was good as she had to keep up with me – and she was very generous; she did a huge amount of charity work, performing in elderly care homes either by herself or with her pupils. The strange thing was, she took her disability so lightly that I never actually thought of her as being disabled. To me she was just like anyone else, but her energy and passion for people made her so different. She truly was unique.

I looked forward to her sessions all week, and every Saturday morning I would pack up my music folder and Mum would drive me over to Mrs Nield's bungalow. Her music room was at the back of the house, overlooking the garden. "Come in! Come in!" she would say cheerily, propelling herself sharpish to the door in her wheelchair. She loved to chat, and more often than not she'd still be busy with another pupil when I got there, her poor timekeeping meaning that she'd usually be running late. I never minded, though; I always loved looking at all the music awards, old photos, certificates, and diplomas that covered every inch of her walls while I waited.

The room itself was crammed with all things musical; her piano was covered in knickknacks, old trinkets, kitsch ornaments, and an ever-swaying metronome, I'd always stare at it in motion when she wasn't looking:

ick... tick... tick... The metronome beats in time.
.. tick... tick...

Also scattered around the room were various guitars on stands, fronting bookcases and heaving shelves that were stuffed full of sheet music, some having fallen to the floor. It was a wonderful kind of chaos.

The doors leading into the music room all had cat flaps, allowing her pets to come and go whenever they wanted. They pretty much did whatever they wanted too, jumping onto the piano or rubbing themselves up against you.

While Mrs Nield loved her cats, unfortunately I didn't, as I was – and still am – very much allergic to cats and their hair. My eyes would itch and my face would puff up, it sometimes getting so bad that I felt like gouging my eyes out – not something that's conducive to singing and playing instruments. I would mention this to her but she would always forget, and I didn't have the heart to remind her over and over again; she loved those animals like they were her children.

So, whenever they wandered in, purring and fawning, I would just grin and tamely tap them with my feet, effectively shooing them away. It more or less worked, and when it didn't, I just tried to get on with it, no matter how much my eyes were streaming or how puffy my eyes looked. It seems in the singing world, sometimes sacrifices have to be made.

Despite my issues with her cats, it wasn't long before Mrs Nield invited me to join her choir, which I swiftly did. We sang at the local senior care homes, which was fun, but I do remember them smelling strongly of cabbage – yes, singing is a very glamorous profession. You'd always get someone in the 'crowd' who was a little hard of hearing, shouting "When's dinner ready?" or When are they going home?" They were always kind and the music made them smile, which made me and the rest of the choir feel pretty good too. As it turned out, the elderly all loved Abba covers (much like me). What can I say? *Thank You for the Music*... Do I love

Abba?... *I Do, I Do, I Do, I Do.*

This is why I love music.

One day, Mrs Nield sprang a big surprise on me. "I hear your school is having a Folk event tomorrow night, and I want you to perform a song. I'll accompany you on the guitar." She must have seen me tense up, because she quickly added, "You can do it, Vicky. One day I can see you headlining a big show."

My initial reaction was one of embarrassment – though I was flattered, I didn't really believe what she was saying; it's not in my nature to take compliments seriously. Still, I agreed, though somewhat reluctantly – singing in front of a music teacher and her cats is pretty different to singing in front of a crowd of people, especially when that crowd were students in your own school. It was going to be interesting, alright.

On the night of the show, the school assembly hall was full of both teachers and classmates, some of which were new faces to me. Although I was popular at school, I tended to keep myself to myself, and this was the first time I'd really put myself out there'.

While my voice might have been ready, my wardrobe was definitely not – the dress style for the event was country and western to match the music, but I didn't own a cowboy hat, and nothing in my wardrobe had even the slightest bit of fringe on it. I had no choice but to improvise, so I ended up wearing a pair of flared jeans, which was the closest thing I owned that would match the dress code brief. Unfortunately, they didn't fit very well – so much so that the fly didn't fully go up. Fortunately, I was also wearing one of Mum's old red checked shirts, which due to it being twice my size, covered the gaping hole in my jeans thanks to the un-done button. What a nightmare – enter stage right; cow girl takes to centre stage dressed in strange, oversized clothes...

I was feeling nervous, but I soon got into the song, and when I finished, the whole assembly hall stood up, applauding me and stamping their feet. I could feel myself going red, and to add to my awkwardness, the headmaster jumped onto the stage and told everyone how impressed he was with my performance – he proclaimed that I was a 'star in the making'. Back then I was painfully shy, and I hid my face behind the sheet music on my music stand. Still, more than anything I felt a sense of relief – that I'd got through the song, and that I'd done it without my oversized jeans falling down and exposing my knickers!

Over the next few years, as well as taking my music exams, I sang in lots of music festivals and talent shows, gaining experience wherever I could.

One event I attended consisted of vocalists and musicians from all over Cheshire meeting up in schools during the summer holidays to compete in classical singing competitions. Each classroom would be packed with talented youngsters, showing off their musical skills and voices, and you wouldn't believe how competitive these things were. God! It was cut-throat – microphones and violin bows at dawn!

Basically, you had to perform in front of a panel of extremely stern-faced judges, as well as hordes of precocious child performers and their pushy parents. I would get nervous and queasy every time – it was far scarier than performing in front of my school. Still, I would always get through it, and once I'd sung, I knew that I'd survived. It was such a great sensation, it made me feel invincible.

I was good enough to win some of the events, meaning that I got to carry off prestigious sliver trophies – huge cups and shields that were decades old and steeped in history. While I loved singing and all the attention it brought me, winning was more about the challenge for me – if I didn't win, I was never too bothered, never too disappointed. As I saw it, if I'd tried my best, then what more could I do?

Looking back, even at the age of 9 or 10 it was clear that I had a very sensible and balanced approach to what made me happy. It was only when I got older – when things weren't turning out exactly as I'd hoped – when I got told I wasn't trying hard enough; this was when my approach to music started to change.

INT. JED'S HOLLYWOOD HILLS HOME. DECK CANYON VIEW. SLIDING DOORS TO DECK. DAYTIME - SUNNY

VICKY walks towards the glass sliding doors and takes in the view across the canyon, she then cautiously looks around and then carefully slides the doors open. JED, upstairs hears the deck doors opening.

JED. Shouts down from upstairs (irritated)

                    JED
No!! shut the doors, I've told you before Vicky... Keep my cats in! I don't want them on the decks outside... I've told you before, those birds will peck em.up! I told you! I hate them Kites!

VICKY quickly blocks the bottom of the open doors with her feet - stopping the cats in their tracks trying to escape outside. She closes the doors quietly. Her expression - submissive, looking found out.

                    VICKY
   Ok JED, Sorry... I've shut them!...
         Pesky cats... (whispered)

VICKY turns her head and looks up towards the stairs - a blank expression.

                    JED
          Thank You!! (loudly)

FADE OUT:

I was 14 when I got spotted at a charity singing competition, where – unbeknown to me – a talent scout for a major theatrical company was in the audience. Some weeks later, I remember walking downstairs just as the phone rang. The way my Mum was talking made me pause, and when she saw me hovering in the kitchen, she placed the receiver on her chest and whispered, "V…Vicky, it's a theatre producer… she wants you to audition for a show at the Manchester Lowry!"

At first, I thought I'd misheard her. "The Lowry? Mum… really? You're joking!"

She shook her head, a little laugh escaping from her lips. "I'm not! It's for the lead role in *Sleeping Beauty.*"

"*WHAT!!!*" Yes, that was pretty much my response.

It sounded wonderful and amazing, but the truth was, I was scared and unsure. The Lowry theatre was a big deal, and *Sleeping Beauty* was also a big production to take on. Despite my fears, however, my competitive streak kicked in and I knew that I wanted to at least try for it – I had to be in with a chance.

This chance had come about after the girl chosen to play the lead part in *Sleeping Beauty*, Heidi Range, had quit the show to join the pop group, the Sugababes. The thing that concerned me most was that Heidi was 19 and I was only 14. I was a baby, and a baby-faced baby at that! I'd never done anything like this before - maybe I was too young for the part – I just really wasn't sure about it at all. One thing I *was* sure of, however, was that the challenge would be daunting. Extremely daunting.

At around that time, I'd also come to the conclusion that I was starting to outgrow Mrs Nield's singing lessons; although I enjoyed them and thought she was wonderful, I felt that she'd taken me technically as far as she could, so I stopped going to her classes. I needed a change – a challenging, new direction – and therefore new coaches and teachers were needed too.

Mrs Nield and I parted on friendly terms, but that didn't stop me from feeling guilty, both due to the fact that she wouldn't be tutoring me anymore, and that she would miss out in sharing all the excitement. After all, I'd been going to her for lessons since the age of eight, and now that things were happening, I was leaving. I felt a little disloyal to say the least.

The audition for *Sleeping Beauty* was being held in a week's time at the Lowry Theatre in Salford Quays, Manchester, and as it was a school day, I needed the headmaster's permission to attend. I was a little nervous about asking, but they said yes without hesitation, and my classmates couldn't have been more pleased for me – even though they'd never really heard me sing, they were incredibly supportive nonetheless.

All week long I practised my two favourite songs – *Immortality* by Celine Dion and *Don't Rain on My Parade* by Barbra Streisand – plus a song from the show that the producer wanted me to learn called *Live for The One I Love*. All three were big, belting, powerhouse show tunes that demanded strength and stamina, and I knew that if I did them well, they'd impress the people I needed to impress.

On the morning of the audition I thought long and hard about what to wear – bearing in mind that I was auditioning to replace a 19-year-old young woman, I needed to look as grown-up as possible. To this end, I chose a tight-fitting burgundy turtle neck that clung to my boyish frame and emphasised what little curves I had at the time. I paired the jumper with my only fashionable item, my pride and joy – a pair of Miss Sixty flared jeans, which I'd bought using the money I'd won after coming third to a rock band in a talent competition run by the Manchester Evening News a few months before. They were very expensive and had a rather conspicuous Father Christmas type belt buckle. To complete the ensemble, I slipped on a pair of clunky 90's style ankle boots, which gave the impression that I was taller than I actually was. I then made myself highly inflammable by dousing half a can of hair spray *all* over my head, coughing and spluttering in the process. As Dolly Parton once famously said. *"The higher the hair, the closer to heaven,"* Amen to that.

When the time came, Mum drove me to the Lowry, and just as we were cruising along the M60 motorway, I was suddenly gripped by an old, familiar friend: stage fright. It happened most times when I was setting off for an audition or a performance, but even after experiencing it so many times, it was always as horrible as it was expected – a sickening feeling that churned my stomach, like I had a million butterflies fluttering around in there. Add to that some clammy hands, and soon I was experiencing the worst of all fears – self-doubt!

This time, though, faced with the enormity of what I was about to do, it seemed ten times worse, crushing me like an avalanche as I stared out of the car window. My hands shook slightly, my head pounded, and my mouth felt as dry as sandpaper. I started to cough, convinced that I'd lose my voice if I didn't clear my throat properly, so I'd cough again, making my throat even more dry. Throughout all of this I was running lyrics around in my head, repeating them over and over again, convinced that if I didn't, I'd forget them. It was driving me mad, a cornering attack.

Surely disaster lay ahead! I decided that I needed an escape route, and fast.

"Mum," I said, my voice panicked. "Turn the car around."

"What, why?" came the shocked reply.

"I don't feel well. I want to go home."

Luckily, my Mum had gone through this same scenario with me many times before, and she knew exactly what to say. "Just relax, Vicky. Everything's going to be fine…do you remember when you sang and played Alice at school, in Alice in Wonderland… the school play, you were only ten then!?... Yeah, now that worked out fine didn't it?"

"Yes," I said, thinking back. (revelation).

Her reassuring words did the trick – all I needed was a little validation, a little encouragement, it was the same every time. I was soothed, so soothed in fact that I closed my eyes, thinking, where should I go? ……. well, that depends on where you want to end up! and before I knew it…

"Here we are!" Mum blurted out.

GOSH!! I opened my eyes and saw this crazy-shaped building rushing towards me, a modernist, stainless steel and glass structure. Was I really going to sing in there? This was no school stage or tiny room – this was a huge place.

A few moments later, Mum stopped the car in front of the theatre. The building looked down at me, impressive and intimidating.

My nerves jangling, I grabbed my bag containing my music and got out of the car. I walked towards the building, and as I stepped into the foyer, a strange feeling came over me: for once, I actually felt like a professional singer, like I was making my grand entrance. Apart from my legs feeling like jelly, it felt like I had arrived.

I gave my name at reception and was told to make my way to the Quay's Theatre. Once there, I quietly made my way into the theatre through two pairs of soundproofed doors, revealing a cavernous two-tiered auditorium bathed in semi-darkness, with rows and rows of seats plunging steeply down towards the stage, there was a deadening silence. I felt tiny.

The theatre was empty apart from two people – the director, Viv, and her husband. They welcomed me with a smile and greeted me in their soft Scouse accents. Nothing much was said, just the pleasantries; like most auditions, it was clear that they wanted to keep me intrigued and on my toes.

"Right," said Viv. "Let's hear you sing."

I handed my music to Viv's husband and then climbed the steps onto the stage. I stood there for a moment, feeling incredibly small in the vast space, hoping that my wobbling legs wouldn't be visible to the two-people staring at me.

The stage was lit by overhead lights, and there was a single spotlight directed on me, the singer. The star. I squinted up at the stalls, but they were just a blur – they may as well have been miles away. At that moment, I felt just like Barbra Streisand in the musical film, *Funny Girl*. I took a sharp deep breath and got myself composed and under control.

Viv and her husband stared at me, waiting.

It was time.

The moment I started to sing, my nerves vanished, and I belted out all three songs both word and pitch perfect. The acoustics were out-of-this-world, my voice soaring all the way up to the Gods. It felt incredible – *I* felt incredible.

After my performance, I was handed a script and told to act and read a few lines from it. I knew this was coming, but I still felt unsure – apart from school drama classes - Alice in Wonderland - and a few makeshift plays I'd done at home with family and friends, I'd never read from a proper script before. Still, I was confident I could pull it off; I'd seen my fair share of Disney movies and I knew how to play a damsel in distress.

By the time the audition came to an end, my adrenaline was pumping. My nerves and stage fright gone, I was happy with my performance and I felt that I'd given it my best shot. What else could I do?

Viv thanked me and said she would be in touch, giving away absolutely nothing as I said my goodbyes.

On the drive home, I told Mum all about it, and after staring at me for a few seconds, she hesitantly asked, "Well... do you think you've got the part?"

I shrugged my shoulders, trying to look calm even though deep inside I was a volcano of expectation. "I'm not sure. Let's just see what happens."

Two days later, the phone rang and Mum answered. I knew straight away that it was Viv on the other end, and I held my breath as I listened to the one-sided conversation.

After the phone call, Mum turned to me and smiled.

I'd got the part. Wow!! – £40 per show – Kerching! -- I was in the money!

INT OF CAR. RIFFS MUSIC SCHOOL. STOCKPORT.
NIGHT.

KEVIN (VICKY'S DAD) and VICKY are sat
outside the music school in the car. VICKY
is late for a recording session and refusing
to go in. VICKY is tearful - there's a
heated argument.

FADE IN :

                    KEVIN
You're just not trying hard enough. You're
  letting yourself down and everyone else.
  This is why it's not happening for you.

                    VICKY
                  (shouting)
I'm sick of this… You always blame *me*! You
   have NO idea how hard I try, how much
   effort I put in, how much I want this

                    KEVIN
            GET OUT! Just get out…

                    VICKY
   Fine, pull over. I can't stand you. You
           can just **** off!

                      34

VICKY makes a grab for the door handle and storms out of the car. KEVIN tries to grab VICKY'S arm as she gets up out of the car seat - she manages to shrug him off. VICKY walks off and KEVIN follows her in the car by the side of the pavement with the window down

                    KEVIN
                   (angry)
Get back in the car, don't be silly, we're
   miles away from anywhere... Get back in
                    now,
              it's DARK!

                    VICKY
             (crying, screaming)
Go away... Just leave me alone... Go away!

CUT TO :

I couldn't believe it – I was cock-a-hoop; I felt excited, lifted, and terrified all at the same time. I ran upstairs to my bedroom, closed the door, and thought, 'Yes! Yes! I've got it! I've got it!'

This elation was short-lived, however, as my next thought was: 'Oh Crap! I've actually got to do it now!' Dark, negative thoughts soon closed in, sending me into a panic as I thought: 'No, no, I can't do this. I can't play the lead role in a professional musical! It's ridiculous! Seven weeks! Two shows a day! With all those people watching me and judging me? It won't work! I'm only 14! What were they thinking? They must be out of their minds!'

After the panic, I ran downstairs to talk it over with my mum and dad. I started rambling, pouring out all the negative thoughts I'd been having, and after listening to me, they sat me down and talked it through with me. They were caring and supportive, telling me that it was my big chance and that I would have so much fun doing it, which was the main thing. It was exactly what I needed to hear, and in the end, all my negative thoughts evaporated. The excitement was back.

Over the next two weeks, Mum and Dad drove me to and from rehearsals, giving me all sorts of parental advice about not leaving the theatre on my own and of being aware of the people around me at all times. Strangely enough, I was more nervous about rehearsals than I was about doing the actual show.

I was introduced to the cast and crew and I tried my best to get on with them –they were all professionals, after all. The oddest part, though, was meeting Prince Charming; he was in his early twenties, which to a girl my age seemed old. I mean, boys my age didn't even have facial hair yet, and here was this grown-up man who had to pretend to be my prince! Unnatural was not the word.

The first time he kissed me on stage was a little awkward; he smelled of aftershave, another difference with boys my age. Luckily, I was 'asleep' and didn't really have to act like I was enjoying it – a big relief.

I'm pleased to say that the cast took me under their wing and that we soon became one big happy family – we'd hang out after rehearsals and go to dinners and parties together. One night, I got invited out by some of the cast to a club in Manchester's Gay Village, and my first thought was that I needed a new set of clothes. My wardrobe at the time consisted of fleeces and *Adidas* tracksuit bottoms – hardly suitable attire for a leading lady out on the town.

I spent a hundred quid of my earnings on clothes from the Lowry outlet, and we all had a fab evening out. There I was, dancing the night away while my schoolmates were all tucked up in bed ready for an early morning of packing up textbooks and doing last minute homework.

Looking back now, it was all a bit haze – how I managed to get into some of those clubs, I have no idea. Even today I get asked for ID for proof of age, most embarrassingly for buying paracetamol. It's safe to say that I grew up a lot during that time; it was a real coming of age period for me. For one thing, it was the first time I stayed out late and got tipsy. I knew that I was always in safe hands though, as I was well looked after by the older members of the cast. It made me feel more mature, like I belonged in that world. It felt grown up.

The days leading up to 'first night' were hectic – it was a blur of costume fittings and dress rehearsals. As each member of the cast had to do their own make-up, Mum and I trawled around Boots to stock up on crayon-like-foundation, pearly lip gloss, pink blusher, and many, many cans of *Elnett* hairspray, the smell of which even to this day reminds me of the show.

I got to the Lowry early on opening night, and the theatre was buzzing – lighting and sound engineers doing last minute checks, cast members rushing around backstage, the producer and director standing in a huddle, swapping notes. It suddenly hit me at that moment that all of these people were relying on me. Me! I was a 14-year-old schoolgirl headlining a big show, a thought that occasionally reared its head and made me feel sick inside. What if I messed up? What if I forgot my lines and made a complete fool of myself? I'd never live it down!

Snapping back to reality, I told the Darth Vader voice of fear in my head to shut up – it was far too late to worry about that now. For one thing, the show was sold out, and for another, lots of my family and friends were coming, not to mention all the local press. It didn't bear thinking about, so I tried not to think about it. I'd learnt my lines, I'd perfected the songs, and I was ready to go. Bring it on!

My bravado slowly ebbed away, however, as the call came over the backstage tannoy: "Ten Minutes, ten minutes!" I was sharing a dressing room with two other members of the cast, and gradually, one by one, they left to take their place on stage. I didn't appear until the second act, so I had to sit by myself for a good ten minutes, staring at my overly made-up face in the mirror and listening to the opening act of the show through the speaker system.

Once again, my heart began to pound and my throat started to tighten. I glanced at the fire exit, and the thought suddenly occurred to me: what if? What if I suddenly got up, pushed open the door, and ran off into the night? No one could physically stop me, could they? If I did that – if I made a run for it – all this pressure would be over. I could just grab a taxi and go home. - If life was only so simple!

Then something kicked in – confidence, willpower, guilt, I don't know – and I started to calm down. I knew of course, that running wasn't an option, and I would never let all of those people down – it was just another stage in my ever-increasing stage fright. But I'd got past it.

I heard my cue, got up, and made my way to the side of the stage, all in a bit of a daze. The second act had now started, and from the darkened wings I saw the stage blazing with light, my fellow cast members cavorting around, their costumes shimmering. It was magical. Otherworldly. I couldn't quite believe that I was a part of it, that in one step – one tiny step – I would join them.

According to the script, Sleeping Beauty makes her entrance on a skateboard (she was a rather modern Princess, after all) and when my cue came, I grabbed the skateboard off the prop man, placed my left foot on it, and propelled myself onto the stage.

I'm proud to say that it was a flawless opening night. There were no slip-ups, no disasters, nothing. I remembered all of my lines and I sang each song with both power and control. As usual, once I was on that stage, my niggling doubts and my nerves vanished.

As the curtain fell, the audience rose to their feet and gave us a standing ovation whilst the rest of the cast and I danced around the stage to *Don't Stop Me Now* by Queen. The thrill walking to the front of the stage and taking a bow after a fantastic performance is indescribable – one of the best ever. The director and producer stood in the wings, beaming, and I was so happy that I hadn't let them down. The adrenaline was amazing – I wanted it again, and again, and again.

The rest of the evening was a bit of a blur. After a rousing curtain call my parents and sisters rushed backstage to congratulate me. Of course, to stop me from getting too carried away and ahead of myself, my Dad looked at me and said, "Well done, Vicky. Only another seven weeks to go!" He was right. Two shows a day lay ahead, but I was more than ready for the challenge. I had nailed the opening night, and I couldn't be happier or more prepared for what was to come.

There was a backstage party but I didn't stay long; I just wanted to go home and be with my family. As I was leaving through the stage door, however, I was besieged by a crowd of very cute small children and grinning teenagers, all of whom were keen for me to autograph their programs. It was so weird! Blushing, I signed each one, all the time thinking how unreal it felt, as though it was happening to someone else. 'God!' I thought, 'this is what stardom must be like!'

As much as I loved the attention and praise, for the most part the spotlight made me feel a little bit uncomfortable; I was so desperate to be liked and understood that I overthought everything I did for fear of being criticised. How I dressed, the make-up I wore, what I said, the choices I made… everything.

Whenever I doubted myself, I would think, 'act like your favourite pop stars' or 'what would Christina do?' I had very little faith in my own being – I was still testing the waters, constantly reshaping my personality and demeanour. It's hard to know how to act when, deep down, you know you really shouldn't be acting at all.

Behind the flurry of smiley children at the stage door, I spotted someone right at the back of the crowd, sitting patiently in her wheelchair: Mrs Nield. It was a chilly night and she was wrapped up in a scarf, looking absolutely freezing. I'd not seen her since we'd parted company a few months ago, so as I walked over to her, I was unsure of the reaction I'd get.

I needn't have worried. She smiled, took my hand, and said, "I'm so proud of you, Vicky. You were marvellous. Amazing! I said one day you would headline a big show and I was right." Before she left, she handed to me a small hand tied bouquet of pink roses, inside the bouquet was a hand-written card.

"A bouquet for the star on her opening night. Let your voice soar and the audience will soar with you. All my love, Mrs Neild"

I was so touched that she'd made the effort to come and see the show, especially on such a freezing cold night. What an amazingly kind and generous lady.

A few years ago, I heard the very sad news that Mrs Nield had passed away. I thought back to all the hours I'd spent in her company; her patience, her kindness, but most of all, her wisdom. All her life she'd battled against pain and disability, and yet never once did I hear her complain. She truly was an inspiration, and words alone cannot express the debt I owe her.

She started me on my singing path, teaching me everything she knew, but most importantly, she encouraged me to be more than I thought I could be.

She gave me the confidence to go after my dreams.

God bless Mrs Nield… and all her beloved cats.

Glimpses of Me… Scar Tissue

*The tea trolley's squeaky wheel squeaks… and squeaks … and squeaks…
The ward smelt of antiseptic (amongst other things.) I'm in Macclesfield
General Hospital recovering from an operation. I had been back and forth in
here for about month with painful stomach cramps and a fever; it was the
worst pain I've ever experienced. It was so bad I couldn't walk or stand up
straight and had to resort to crawling around like a wounded crab. When
they found out what was wrong with me they told me I didn't have much time
left, I needed an emergency operation. It was peritonitis. A burst appendix.
It sounded messy.*

Here's the nurse now. She looks like she's heading my way.

"Morning, Vicky. Feeling better today?"

"I'm ok but my stitches in my stomach are still really sore."

"That's normal. You'll soon be better and back home"

*Another five boring hours of daytime television before lunch and I can't wait.
My sisters are visiting and have promised to bring me a McDonald's Happy
Meal. At least I won't have to eat the hospitals out-of-a-packet mashed
potato and suspect sausages for dinner. I'm feeling happier already!*

Squeak… squeal… squeak… squeal... the tea trolley's back!

INT. FAMILY DINING ROOM. POYNTON. DAY -
RAINING

KEVIN paces the dining room floor, holding
a telephone to is ear

                    KEVIN
  Hello, good morning. Is that the chancery
      division office of the high court?

PAUSE
COURT OFFICER holding a phone.

                COURT OFFICER
      Yes, it is, how may I help you?

                    KEVIN
   Oh good, yes... hope you can help... my
 daughter Vicky, is being sued in the high
 court, and I just wondered if we could get
    legal aid to help fund her defence?

                COURT OFFICER
    Sorry no, there's no legal aid for
          commercial litigation.

                    KEVIN
 Oh, it's just that she's only just 16, and
        she has no money or job...

                    PAUSE - COURT OFFICER furrows his
                         eyebrows, surprised.

                              COURT OFFICER
                              Sixteen?!

                                 KEVIN
                       Yes, she's still at school.

          Small period of silence.

                              COURT OFFICER
                    ...If she's not 18, how can they do that?

          COURT OFFICER looks puzzled.

                                 KEVIN
                       I don't know... You tell me?!

3

The Introduction…

"So, tell us who you're going to be tonight, Vicky?"

The live studio audience waited expectantly. "Tonight, Matthew, I'm going to be... Tina Arena!"

This wasn't a dream; this was really happening. I was stood on stage at ITV studios with Matthew Kelly towering over me. Applause rang out. I turned, walked downstage and waved, disappearing through a set of sliding doors and dry ice. I was fifteen and was about to perform in one of the UK's favourite TV talent show *'Stars in Their Eyes kids special'*. Seconds later, as if by magic, the doors slid open and through a billowing fog I walked onstage transformed: I was TINA! No, not Tina Turner… Aussie goddess Tina Arena. Apparently, it didn't take much to make me look like Tina Arena. I wore a not-so-subtle bouncy, brown wig and brown contact lenses coupled with a long, shapeless, column-like sleeveless gown that I suspect were a fine pair of curtains in a previous life. I'd been chosen to appear on the kid's version of the show after sending in a CD of three songs I'd recorded as a birthday present at a studio experience day in Stockport - It seems it does pay to keep on posting those demos! After sending it to the show on a whim, I was invited for an audition. The next thing I knew, I got an offer to sing on the show; I was surprised and chuffed to bits knowing I was going on the telly.

The transformation from freckled schoolgirl to musical diva was incredibly fun. I got three days off school (which was a bonus) and I went to London for the day for a wig fitting and rehearsed with the show's choreographer. The next two days were spent at ITV Studios in Manchester – one day to rehearse, including a run-through with the crew and other contestants, the next day to film the actual show, which happened to fall on my 15th birthday. I remember Matthew presenting me with a cake in front of the whole crew whilst singing Happy Birthday. It was certainly a birthday I would remember for a long time. One of my fellow contestants was Aston Marigold, who later went on to join JLS. There was another girl who was performing as Jennifer Lopez. She looked great in her tight, fitted jeans and hoop earrings, looking all sexy in her J-Lo-esque get-up whilst singing about how "*Love Don't Cost a Thing.*" I looked like something from the museum of ugliness: with my bouffant brown wig and brown contacts washing me out like a deathly ghost. When you're 15 you want to start experimenting with style and femininity. I clearly had got off to a slow start. On the bright side, at least I had a great song, now *that* was something I had going for me. The song was big and powerful and it was a really beautiful song to sing. It was a showstopper… I've always been drawn to songs that power along, taking you emotionally on a journey.

I approached the microphone through a haze of blue, spotlights puncturing the mist like searchlights. I sang the first bars of *Whistle Down the Wind* from the musical of the same name. More cued applause. Despite being nervous and a having a cluster of TV cameras trained on me, I managed to give a perfect performance, hitting every note and remembering every line. The studio audience clapped and cheered led no doubt by mum and dad who I told to give a few whoops and whistles! Once again, I'd got to sing on a proper stage. There's no feeling like it. The adrenaline. The attention. The control. I loved it, I wanted more of it.

Matthew Kelly walked back onstage, smiling and nodding his head in approval. "Well, Vicky," he gushed. "That was amazing! Wasn't it, ladies and gentle........."

The TV screen went blank. William Robinson, my prospective manager switched off the TV we were all watching, and put down the TV remote control and got to his feet. He began pacing the room thoughtfully. "Now then! Now then!" he exclaimed, "What have we here… what have we here? You look fantastic on TV… What was the name of that song? I want to watch it again"

"Whistle Down the Wind" I said.

I was sitting in the lounge of his house in deepest rural Cheshire having just watched a video of my appearance on 'Stars in Their Eyes'. William had invited me over to discuss a management proposal; he wanted to be my manager, although I didn't know it at that time, his cool demeanour gave nothing away. Rolling green fields and dairy farms surrounded the house from where he worked. The type you'd see on 'Escape to The Country'. Mum and Dad were sitting either side of me on a huge black leather sofa; a calm, protective presence. Everything about the room screamed 'bachelor pad' – dark lighting, chunky furniture littered with fast-food containers and coffee-stained mugs, not to mention the world's largest TV – Unwashed dishes and glasses piled high in the sink, pizza boxes littering the worktops and an empty KFC bargain bucket standing on the table – maybe a heavy night with the band?

A lanky young guy with long greasy hair and pale complexion hovered around us awkwardly as we sat and talked. His name was Paul, William's sound engineer and go-too man.

"Would anyone like a drink?" asked Paul.

As Paul took our drink orders, William said, "Cheers, Cell."

Dad and I looked at one another, confused. When Paul closed the door, dad asked William what he meant by 'Cell'.

"Paul's only got one brain cell. Hence 'Cell'.' We all laughed, uncomfortably, I think he thought he was being witty.

When the drinks arrived, William invited us to his ground floor office. It was the kind of room you'd expect an agent/promoter to inhabit, a room where all kinds of deals are cooked up. The walls were plastered with framed photos of the many artistes he'd represented and promoted – smiling singers and edgy looking rock bands, nostalgic soul groups and z-list celebrities; some I'd heard of, some I hadn't. He pointed out each one in turn, giving us the lowdown on their careers – sometimes funny. A large writing desk inlaid with green leather stood in one corner of the room, behind which was a smart leather chair peppered with brass studs. On the desk were two enormous PC screens, a keyboard and a guitar shaped mouse. – I should of ran right of there!

You're all just the same, Too good to be true
You promise it all, But you don't have a clue
Mr So Sure, Laid back all talk
All games big tease, Big fake all dreams

William gestured proudly to a wall of framed and signed Manchester United football shirts. He told us he had a lot of connections at the club, this pleased Dad, he was well impressed. William then took us back into the lounge where we all sat round the coffee table. The conversation switched from friendly chit-chat to a more business-like tone.

"OK, said William. "Let's cut to the chase. I think Vicky's a very talented singer. I'd love to represent her, subject to proper contracts of course. I've had a word with my lawyers and they said the best way for us all to move forward is for Vicky to enter into two business agreements with my partners and me. With the right management on board I think she could get to the very top."

I felt out of my depth. This wasn't just me singing at charity shows for fun anymore, this was something more serious. I wanted to take the leap of faith but it felt unnerving. As much as I felt like I was ready to step up to the plate, I didn't yet feel brave enough to put my heart on the line. When you're young you still have the power of ignorance, you can be flippant and change your mind if you want to. But this would mean commitment and maybe something more life changing. It would be a serious decision, no more ill-considered schoolgirl. Mum and Dad looked concentrated and thoughtful, taking in everything he said. I had the feeling they were a little daunted themselves. They had the same look as a Deal or No Deal contestant who must gamble on the 50/50 board. We were just an ordinary family with no experience of the entertainment industry. This was new ground for us.

"They'll be two contracts to sign," continued William. "A management agreement and a production agreement. Now, the contracts will need to be drawn up by a specialist entertainment lawyer in London. Only the best music and entertainment lawyers are based there. This industry's very London centric." He went on to explain that the contracts would be complex to draft because a minor was party to them (i.e. me). "Vicky's only 15 you see, not 18." Mum and Dad nodded as if they knew this, which in fact they didn't… they knew I was 15 though! I didn't say anything in case I sounded silly. As a strong-minded teenager, this was hard for me to do, keep quiet. Besides, I wasn't really used to conversing confidently with middle-aged men, especially someone like William, his confident swagger seemed a bit put on, a bit fake. Let's face it, to be fair to him, it takes a lot for anybody to impress and blag a teenager. I was guarded to all strangers, they had to earn my trust. I had very high ideals. I remember feeling cautious and thinking maybe we were getting in way above our heads. But that's the thing about the music business, it bedazzles you, it lures you in and you do get in above your head.

William leant forward on the sofa. "Obviously the contracts have to be fair to both parties. This is something I absolutely insist upon." He paused, staring at Mum and Dad. "Everything needs to be above board, with absolutely no undue influence whatsoever, it has to be fair to both sides"

For some reason during our chat he kept repeating this phrase over and over again – 'No undue influence whatsoever'. It was like a mantra. That, and the word 'absolutely'. It made me quietly giggle. William got up and disappeared into his office. I looked at Mum and Dad optimistically, trying to work out what they were thinking. Both had straight faces, silently weighing up the pros and cons of the offer. I caught Dad's eye and his mood lightened. He smiled, giving me a reassuring nod.

William bounced back into the room, handed dad a piece of paper which listed London's top entertainment lawyers.

While Dad studied the list, we chatted about Sheila Gott, one of my singing coaches who had recommended me to William. Sheila primarily taught pop singing, which was totally different from the strict classical lessons I'd had in the past. It was fun and I loved that I could excel at singing in a Pop style – something I'd not been allowed to do before. I was told it would get me into bad habits apparently. She saw how ambitious I was and gave my demos to William. YouTube or Myspace wasn't around yet so passing on your demos to those 'in the know' was the only way aspiring artistes knew of getting heard.

Dad piped up, "This law firm looks good – Cook Eaglet."

Just to emphasise Dad's naivety about the music business he told me later that he'd chosen this particular law firm because it had the least number of names in its title, unlike the pretentious triple or quadruple-barrelled ones you usually see on polished brass plaques outside fancy head offices.

Dad then asked how much the lawyers would charge for drawing up the contracts.

"Oh, about a £1000," said William, in a matter-of-fact way. "But don't worry, I'll make sure there's a clause in the contracts that means that this will be paid to you as an advance to cover all legal fees."

This seemed agreeable and I was relieved that dad didn't have to fork out a thousand pounds out of his own pocket. He'd paid out enough for me over the years. I would feel so awful if it all went tit's up and Dad's money had gone down the drain. (Prophetic).

We made our way to the front door and said our goodbyes to 'Cell', who gave us a friendly wave.

There were friendly handshakes and warm hugs all round, which I found a bit cringe. I'm not really a kissy-kissy, touchy-feely kind of a person and it felt even more unnatural at 15 years old. I was pretty sure the evening had been a success. It all felt promising and even though it was all scary and unexpected, it felt great to have someone rooting for me in my corner. William seemed to have connections in the music business and he seemed passionate about wanting to make things happen for me. As hopeful as I was, the cynic in me wasn't truly convinced. Until I can see it, I can't believe it. I didn't feel as if I'd made a connection with William yet. He thought before he spoke and something felt awkward. Mind you, what fifteen-year-old *does* have a connection with a middle-aged man she had just met? I tried to think positively. Here was someone who believed in me, who was willing to manage me and put in all the hard graft. It's a scary thought, placing your life in the hands of a stranger, one man, the key man. But I closed my eyes and put any doubts I had to the back of my mind. I looked at it like this - he seemed fair, a good guy, and I felt for now, I could trust him.

William opened the front door and wished us a safe trip home. "Night, night Superstar, you're gonna be amazing!"

I got into the car, praise and compliments ringing in my ears. Not that they went to my head. Not for one second did I think 'Wow! I've made it, I don't know why I'm like that, but I am. I'm ambitious yes, but I like to understate things and tread carefully. Maybe it was how I was brought up and the fact that I had very down-to-earth parents.

I went to school the next day and got on with my every-day life. Nevertheless, I had the feeling there was an adventure to come, I was about to start a journey into the unknown.

Glimpses of Me… Check-Out the Girl

Baked beans – beep! – Washing powder – beep! – Carrots – beep!

The supermarket conveyer belt never seems to end.

I swear I could do this job in my sleep. That's me, there: the smiley girl sitting behind the check-out till on aisle 9 at Tesco. My back aches and my feet are stone cold – a freezing wind blows through the sliding glass entrance doors every time they open, which is all bloody the time!

God, I hate this uniform; the trousers make me look two stone heavier, and with no waist whatsoever.

"Spillage on dairy! Spillage on dairy! Clean up team required!" the announcement whines in my ears. Then it's back to the muzak – not 'Bryan Adams, Summer of 69' again! How I wish they'd change the record!

'I got my first real six-string

Bought it at the five-and-dime!'

Course you did, Brian. The next line should be:

'Now I'm a billionaire rock star

I'm so rich I got nothing but time!"

Yeah, time... time. We all have time, too much time to dream…

4

Noodling my lyrics - **eh?**

August 6th 2003 was the hottest day of the year. Under a cloudless sky, the UK basked in temperatures that reached a dizzying 95 degrees. In other words, it was flippin' boiling.

The Nolan clan – me, Dad, and my siblings Harriet, Phillipa, and Alexandra – were on our way to the maternity unit at Stepping Hill Hospital in Stockport to see my new baby sister. As Dad drove along with the radio blaring, his brood were all strapped into the back seats, and all four of us were bubbling with excitement – a far cry from the reaction we'd shared several months prior.

I remember it was a cold and wet December evening. We had all been sitting round the large oak table in the dining room, about to have dinner, when Dad had breezed in, smiling widely and holding a bunch of supermarket best-buy flowers for Mum. That was our first clue that something odd was happening. Dad had bought flowers? How unusual! A secret was most definitely brewing.

Of course, in a family as big as ours, things don't stay secret for long. We also don't stay quiet for long, either.

"What's going on?" I asked, desperate to know. "Come on, you're both acting all coy and… weird!" Being the eldest of my siblings, I've always been the voice of the group, the mother hen… The bossy boots, some might say. And I was speaking for all of us when I demanded to know what was happening.

Mum was acting like a shy 16-year-old who was being

interrogated by a gaggle of overly-nosey mates. It was like she was hesitant at the reaction she was going to receive, which made me even more intrigued.

Finally, she looked up shyly from her dinner and smiled then announced, "I'm pregnant, you're going to have a new baby brother or sister." – most likely a sister if Mum's odds are anything to go by!

What? Pregnant? *Again?!* I didn't expect that. We were a tight-knit group, a merry band of sisters who were closer than the four musketeers. The last thing we needed was another sibling coming along, an outsider who might challenge our cosy family unit!

I realise, of course, that my reaction was immature to say the least, and I'm now ashamed to admit that I wasn't at all happy about the news. Unfortunately, my attitude rubbed off on my siblings, and whilst I was making childish remarks that my parents should have been more careful, the others were in tears, wailing like stray cats at this completely unexpected news. How could they do this to us?!

My parents, however, weren't taking any notice of us: they were both just grinning from ear to ear, oblivious in their little bubble of happiness.

Looking back, I think my reaction was down to a fear of change, rather than any actual desire to keep our family unit from growing. I think we all have moments where change forces us to adapt, forces us to be brave in unfamiliar situations. It's scary, but it happens, and you simply must learn how to get used to it.

You think you're going to lose something that you believe you can't live without, and it's this same fear that has stopped me from reaching for new heights many times over the years: it's that Darth Vader voice in my head that says, 'you're not good enough,' 'what are you thinking?!' 'They'll laugh at you,' 'you'll be disappointed!' or 'you'll fail!' It can be hard, but if you learn to silence the baritone beast in your mind and hold your head up high: positivity will breed positivity. If you learn to be adaptable and embrace change instead of running away from it, I believe you can survive anything that life throws at you. You don't even have to know how to play the game; whatever hand you're dealt; you'll always have a straight flush.

Slowly, as the weeks and months went by and as my Mum started to blossom, getting bigger and bigger by the day, I began to get more used to the idea. Once the morning sickness had subsided, she started to really glow, and not the sweaty kind of glow that you get from throwing up all day; that wonderful Mum-to-be glow.

We all started to get used to the idea of having a little baby bouncing around, and we began to guess whether she would have a boy or a girl, although with our genetics, I think we always knew it was going to be a girl! A boy would have been a different proposition entirely – quite frankly, I'm not sure my dad would know what to do if he had a boy; I think he secretly likes being the only man in the house sometimes.

I can only imagine the kinds of conversations that poor baby must have heard while growing in Mum's tummy – heated talks about deals, loud music, me singing at the top of my lungs, slamming doors, arguments between me and my sisters, fun and laughter, and a whole lot more. I felt sorry for the poor little thing. It wasn't even born yet and it was already being subjected to the craziness of our family!

Now, speeding full pelt towards Stepping Hill Maternity Hospital, everything had changed, and we couldn't wait to meet our new baby sister.

As we drove through the hospital gates, a song came on the radio that was well suited for the occasion – *Bring Me to Life by Evanescence*. That's the magic of music: If you open your ears, and you listen hard enough, it truly is the soundtrack of our lives.

Dad parked and then ran into the reception, his girl band of daughters following excitedly behind. The lady at the desk asked for his name, and when she typed it into the computer, she looked up at Dad and said, "All your daughters have been born here at Stepping Hill. You've been busy!"

Dad beamed back at her. "You could say that!"

Inside the delivery room, we got our first peek at baby Elizabeth. She looked so cute lying in Mum's arms, all wrapped up in a little white blanket. After pushing an 8 -pound bundle into the world, Mum – unsurprisingly – looked a little worn out. She was a champion in my eyes, a loving Mum, who has now just delivered a five-a-side football team.

We all took turns to hold and caress this precious little person, being careful not to wake her after Mum had managed to get her to sleep. We were in awe of her innocence; she was just so fragile and tiny. She had that lovely powdery baby smell that is my favourite smell in the whole world – if I could bottle it, I would. I swear that if you get just a whiff of that scent, your ovaries skip a beat.

I was mesmerised by Elizabeth's pale, translucent skin, her tiny hands and her long, curved eyelashes. Mum smiled proudly as each of us gave her a kiss, passing the tiny bundle between us as gently as we could. We were all so thrilled that it was another girl – we could now officially be a Nolan Sisters tribute act if we ever needed a plan B career-wise.

After a while, a nurse brought in a tray of toast, tea, and juice. Dad and I tucked in while my younger sisters explored the recovery room, inspecting all the equipment and generally messing around. Dad soon called a halt to their shenanigans, telling them to behave and to remember where they were.

When it was time to go, we all hugged Mum and blew kisses to baby Elizabeth from the door, waving goodbye as we left the room. Little Alexandra was the last to leave. She was still our baby too. While she was no longer the youngest, she was definitely still the cutest.

The Nolan clan had now grown to seven - lucky seven – the seven notes on the musical scale, all different.

***

Through a misted upstairs window, I saw my manager's car pull onto the drive. Excited, I ran downstairs, clutching a small holdall containing my stage clothes and make up.

Dad walked into the hall just as I was leaving. "Where's the gig tonight?" he asked.

"A Chinese restaurant in Manchester."

His face straightened a little, and I could almost hear him thinking: *Blimey, what are you doing playing in a place like that? You should be signed to a big label by now, doing proper gigs!*

Naturally, I thought the same thing, but I'd also realised that the path to stardom is a long and complicated one, leading you down some unexpected highways and byways. I was just glad to be on that path, even if I was right at the start.

"A gig's a gig, Dad!" I said cheerily, determined to show him that I wasn't the least bit bothered about playing an unglamorous venue. I could pay my dues, and besides, 'All roads lead to Rome', as the philosophers say!

I got in the car, but instead of heading up the Appian Way as I'd been expecting, my manager decided to take the long way around, motoring down the A6 towards Manchester. His soundman Paul was also with us in the car – or Cell, as he still was affectionately called.

Dusk was falling as we approached Manchester City Centre, its warehouses and apartment blocks silhouetted against a blood red sky. We carried on driving into Middleton, North Manchester, eventually following a sign that took us onto a run-down looking industrial estate.

I thought William had gone the wrong way until he pulled up outside our destination, the Ocean Treasure Chinese Restaurant and Nightclub. I thought it was a rather strange place to build a restaurant, slap bang in the middle of drab grey factories and engineering units, but there it was: a long, two-storey building made of mustard-coloured brick and glass, complete with a huge red pagoda-style entrance stuck to the front. I'd never played anywhere like it.

Inside the strange building, it pleasantly surprised me: there were karaoke rooms, a lounge bar, VIP rooms, and a large restaurant with its own stage, where I would be performing. The interior décor was a conglomerate of East meets West; ultra-modern furniture juxtaposed with paper lanterns and hefty Chinese symbols carved from wood and covered in gold leaf.

The main restaurant was packed; a horde of noisy diners was sitting beneath a king-sized chandelier, set in a three-tiered ceiling hung with fairy lights.

Upon entering the restaurant, I was led by a staff member into a storage room next to the kitchen. It was windowless and dank, with sacks of rice and cardboard boxes emblazoned with Chinese symbols stacked up against the wall. The clatter of woks echoed around the room and the smell of Chinese 5-spice was overpowering – very glam!

I quickly got changed and then stepped onto the stage; it was made from polished timber planks and it felt slightly greasy underfoot. I gazed out at the audience – or should I say diners – and realised that none of them were taking any notice of me; they were far too busy scoffing their salt and pepper squid and devouring their spring rolls. It was apparent, they were there to eat, not to hear someone sing.

My manager – who had taken it upon himself to act as compère – jumped onto the stage and introduced me over the restaurant's PA system. Ebullient and brimming with chutzpah, he did his best to whip the audience into a frenzy. "Ladies and gentlemen, you're in for a real treat tonight! Please put your hands together for a star of the future. Catch her now before she hits the big time… it's Miss Vicky Nolan!" (cue electronic organ.)

The audience didn't react at all; they were so engrossed in their food that even if a human-sized king prawn had walked into the room, they still wouldn't have looked up from their plates. So much for the big intro!

I glanced at Paul the soundman who gave me a thumbs up, and after a moment of silence, the backing track started. There was a short burst of feedback and then the first synthesised bars of Quincy Jones' *You Put a Move on My Heart* kicked in. I gave it my all: the moves, the gestures, the heartfelt pleading, and a few Celine Dion-style pounds to the chest for good measure. I meant every word, and I wanted to get that feeling across to my audience.

If there's one thing I've learnt when performing, it's that it doesn't matter how hard you try, or how well you sing, if the audience are busy eating, there's no way they'll connect with you. It was little me vs. the crispy duck. No contest. I wasn't going to win in this place, not when there was delicious food involved.

I finished the song, and a small ripple of applause broke out (or was it the prawn crackers?) I could tell they were being kind – making a morsel of time for me, the cute teenage girl on the stage – but it's difficult to compete, when sweet and sour is on the bill.

***

"You're on in ten, Vicky... Ready? You look fab."

I smiled my confident smile, hoping that the mask wouldn't slip. "Yeah, I'm good."

I was minutes away from my first ever live gig on national television, and the pressure was most certainly on. I had to deliver a knock-out performance; there was no room for error here.

The programme was called *Loose Lips*, a daytime light entertainment show on Living TV. Hosted by Richard Arnold and Melinda Messenger, it was broadcast from Chiswick Studios, West London.

My Dad, my manager William, and I had taken the Virgin train from Manchester earlier in the day, and as the early start and the whole pressure of the occasion began to take its toll, by mid-morning I felt tired and worn out. I'd been rehearsing *You Put a Move on My Heart* all week with my voice and performance coach, Sheila Gott, practising hour after hour, polishing and refining it until it was faultless. We needed perfection; anything else, I was told, just wouldn't do. This programme was a showcase for my voice, and it was going to be live. We hoped that the exposure on national TV would be the launch pad, opening new doors.

Slightly anxious about the song, I was also a little hesitant about what to wear – it's so hard choosing the right look. My manager suggested a few ideas, and he also set me up with a hair stylist who suggested I crimp and wave my hair to give it an extra bit of oomph.

After *many* heated discussions about my image, I settled on bootleg blue jeans and a fitted purple jacket from French Connection, which had an unusual silver chain belt that was covered in hearts. For the first time in my life I felt 'put together,' but boy was it hard work.

Everyone had an opinion about how I should look: *Wear this, wear that, you look crap, you don't look like a star, you look too small, too young, too fat…* Enough! And to top it all off, William wanted me to wear a Peter Pan-green, beret-style hat with a long peacock feather in it. I couldn't help but think: *is this what pop stars have to deal with on a daily basis?* I might not have known who I was yet, but I was definitely not a girl who wore feather hats – that much I *did* know.

I managed to fit a quick rehearsal in before going live on air, which made me feel slightly better as I wanted to get the sound check right; accurate fidelity, mic set up, and floor and camera positions. I kept repeating to myself: don't be nervous, just enjoy it, Vicky. This is a live vocal and a live TV show!

With the sound check over, I made my way to the Green Room where the other guests were watching the show live on a large LED monitor that sat awkwardly above the complimentary drinks and snacks. The mood was friendly if slightly tense, and we all wished each other well.

Soon I'd be hitting the stage, and I told myself repeatedly that I wasn't nervous. This helped me to keep my cool, and the fast-paced day helped as well, as I'd barely had time to think; since arriving in London I hadn't had a moment to myself, barely time even to visit the loo! – hair, make up, a quick chat with the presenters, going through all the do's and don'ts with the producer, the sound checks… Phew! It was a lot to wrap my head around, leaving me with very little time to obsess over the performance.

Towards the end of the show, a production assistant popped his head around the Green Room door. "Right, Vicky; we're ready to go."

Standing up, I quickly checked my appearance in the mirror, adjusting my clothes and hair, and as the assistant led me out of the room, William nodded his approval.

I followed the assistant through a maze of TV production equipment to the side of the stage, and as I looked out at the studio audience, Dad caught my eye; he'd been asked to make up the numbers in the seats.

As I waited to go on, I felt the hot studio lights baking my skin, and peering through a gap in the stage set, I could see the presenters sitting on their sofa, talking to the camera as they started to wind up the show.

I took a deep breath as Richard Arnold turned to the camera, announcing embarrassingly, with gusto, "And here's Robin Gibb's prodigy, Vicky Nolan, singing *'You Put a Move on My Heart.'* We'll see you tomorrow at six."

This was it: Lights... Camera... Action!

I eased into the song, my voice sounding smooth and full of energy. Despite the long day, there was no hint of red, tired eyes – thank God for concealer. All of the hard work was paying off. You definitely reap what you sow. I could see the audience swaying to the gentle rhythms of the beat, and I knew they were enjoying my singing. When it was over I was relieved – I'd just done my first gig on live TV, it turned out to be a pleasure and I really enjoyed the performance.

However, thinking about this performance, it seems it doesn't really matter whether you're facing the state of the art hi-definition cameras on remote controlled booms in a slick London studio, or if you're peering down at a plateful of chicken chow mein in the middle of a northern industrial estate in a Chinese restaurant; it's all the same stuff really... the same song, the same words, the same performance.

I knew then that wherever I performed, I would always give it my all.

***

We pulled into a car park alongside an unassuming office block. The place was rammed, so we drove back onto the busy high street and eventually found a space opposite a Jewish deli. There was no time for a scrumptious salt beef sandwich, though; we were in Willesden, North West London, on business... music business.

It was a late Autumn afternoon, with falling gold and rust coloured leaves sweeping through the scruffy suburban street. Wrapped in warm coats and scarfs, we made our way to the HQ of Jive Records, the main entrance of which lay halfway along the street. It was pretty low-key – no large corporate signs or flashy décor – unlike some of the major labels I'd had previous meetings at. At the time, Jive Records was the largest independent record label in the world, and thinking about it now, maybe their unassuming building was saying: let your noise be your success.

We were met in the reception by Jive's director of A&R, Dave Wibberley. I'd met Dave before at a business meeting in the swanky Landmark Hotel in Marylebone, and over afternoon tea he'd sounded me out about signing to the label. Yippee! Apparently, after seeing the *Loose Lips* performance on TV and then listening to my Copenhagen demos, he'd become a big fan and was interested in my potential.

"You've got it, Vicky," he'd said, tucking into a second piece of chocolate cake. "I'd like for you to meet Jive's MD, Steve Jenkins."

"OK, I'd be please to," I'd replied, cool as a cucumber. "Let's do it!"

Back at Jive HQ, the receptionist directed us to the boardroom on the third floor, and I trooped up the stairs with William and my management team, stopping for just a second outside the room. I stared at the polished wood and brass nameplate, thinking: *my future lies beyond that door.* I was aged just 16 and It was a brief moment, but it's one I remember vividly.

I stepped confidently into the room, seeing the MD, Steve Jenkins, sitting at a large walnut table. Dave Wibberley took a seat next to him.

Steve stood up and greeted me warmly. I introduced my management team – smiles and handshakes all round – then we each took a seat and got down to business.

Steve was the first to speak; he looked at me and asked, "So, Vicky, where did all this begin? Where did all this singing start from?"

I gave him a mini biog, a quick tour of my musical life so far, all the bus stops, and as we chatted, we discovered we had things in common. For instance, both of us were fans of Billy Ocean (his great voice), and he told me that the song *Caribbean Queen* was known as *European Queen* in Europe - he explained about the different song titles for different territories.

Steve then went on to telling me about the label's current artist roster. Britney Spears and Justin Timberlake were mentioned, big names that made me sit up and take notice. *Wow!* I thought. *This guy is actually connected with Britney and Justin!*

Steve was obviously a key player in the music industry; he had power and influence, and I knew I wanted to work with him.

Over the next few hours, the meeting broadened out, with everyone around the table suggesting ideas and proposals. After a quick break for coffee, we all agreed on a plan to move forward. Legals were given instructions to draw up the contracts, and the A&R department went into action on the project.

I had to take a moment for myself at that boardroom table. I was relieved and bubbling with glee, but I also had to think, to remember this moment, to savour it. This was what I'd been working towards and dreaming about all of my young life, and now it was actually happening. It was becoming a reality.

Things seemed to be coming together nicely – as long as

nothing happened with the deal, that was.

Whatever was going to happen and however my career would pan out, I knew one thing with absolute certainty: I would never forget this moment, and I would never forget that feeling of being right on the brink of something.

My future was looking bright, what could go wrong?

I'm gambling with my soul, got my heart out on my sleeve
If you told me I would win, you know I wouldn't leave
I wish that I knew the rules, cause you're playing games with me
If you told me that I would lose, then I'd set myself free

Glimpses of Me... Don't Mention I Did This!

The red and white Virgin Pendolino train snakes its way into Stockport railway station, the matrix sign on the side of the carriage reading 'Destination: London Euston'.

This is mine, so I hop on and grab a seat, soon getting settled. Some minutes into the journey I catch sight of the conductor making his way towards me, inspecting tickets. I'm pensive but strangely excited as that mischievous voice we all have inside our heads sparks into life: Go on, Vicky, I dare you. Richard Branson won't mind. You're a poor twenty-something with no money who's helplessly and madly in love. Mr Branson will understand and he owes you a free train ride anyway – for the one they cancelled on you, ruining your day!

The conductor wishes me good morning, then takes my ticket and crimps it, officiously in blue ink. As soon as his backs turned I innocently lick the ink off the ticket before it dries, hoping nobody notices, which no one does – nobody pays any attention. Great! A free ride, and that's one in the eye for the 'system'. We're even now.

I settle back into my seat, smiling at a herd of cows in a passing field. Warning! Mad woman in seat 12A!

Anyway, I had to do this, I'm skint and on my way to see my lovely boyfriend, Ed,

He's waiting for me at London Euston, standing on platform 10, see, see...

"The things we do for love!"

INT OF CAR. M40 MOTORWAY SERVICE STATION.
THAME OXFORDSHIRE - WEATHER CLOUDY

KEVIN (VICKY'S DAD) and WILLIAM (VICKY'S
MUSIC MANAGER) and VICKY stop at the
motorway service station for fuel and
refreshments. They all buy drinks and ice
cream. WILLIAM and KEVIN both holding and
eating their ice cream cones get back into
the car. They start the car and leave, re-
joining the motorway heading south to
London on the M40. The atmosphere *is* jolly;
the ice creams are melting.

                    KEVIN
    How long before we make London Will?

                   WILLIAM
    About an hour... if the M4'S not busy...
                     the
    meeting's scheduled for 4pm, so we should
                   be ok.

KEVIN and William carry on eating their ice
creams, driving in the fast lane of the
motorway.

                    KEVIN
    We look like a right pair of Wally's
                holding these
    ice creams while driving... (laughing)

WILLIAM

Absolutely... like kids! (laughing)

KEVINS phone rings, he takes it out of his coat, his wife's name APRIL is displayed on the front of the phone, he answers it.

KEVIN

Hi April,... (cheerfully)

APRIL

Hi Kev, where's Vicky?!

KEVIN

She's sat in the back of the car listening to her music on her headphones.

KEVIN turns around as he says this, and looks towards to the back of the car - the seats are empty, and VICKY is not there!

KEVIN

SHIT!!... Where is she? (Alarmed and shocked)

APRIL

You've forgotten her, you idiot!... and left
her back on the motorway at the petrol station!
(angry). She's just called me from the

petrol station
on their phone, her phone is in the car
with you!

WILLIAM spots the motorway traffic sign -
next exit 14 miles!

5

Oath and first verse

"Miss Nolan, please place your right hand on the Bible and take the oath: "'I swear to God that the evidence I shall give shall be the truth, the whole truth, and nothing but the truth.'"

I was standing in the dock at Manchester High Court, looking at all the poker-faced lawyers lined up on the wooden benches in front of me. They were staring at me, – already challenging me, doubting me, before I'd even said a word.

> **"The first thing we do, let's kill all the lawyers"**
> **– William Shakespeare**

You might think that an eighteen-year-old girl fresh out of school who was being forced to stand trial would be nervous, but today I wasn't; I was simply angry and upset, sick to my stomach that my family was being put through such a stressful ordeal, it stank! I'd learnt a great deal about litigation and grown up a lot in the past two years.

This wasn't a singing gig, but it was definitely a performance I was well prepared for: it was all down to me to put the record straight. No matter what happened, I had to make things right again. It was all on me, and I was ready for it.

After repeating the oath in a loud, clear voice, I glanced over at my Mum and Dad sitting in the public gallery. They looked pensive and tired, their faces worn. I could tell they were putting on brave faces, trying their best to look like they were doing OK, even though I knew otherwise. My heart went out to them, I felt responsible.

For the past two years it seemed like we'd been toyed with and thrown around by the justice system, a process that we had trusted and put all our faith in. That trust, so far, had let us down over and over again, with the lawyers seemingly moving the goalposts at every opportunity and wrong footing everybody at our expense.

It shouldn't have got to this, I thought. We are made to believe that we can rely on our legal system to be fair, when really, it's just a giant parasite sucking all the money out of the little guys with no concern for the people involved. Stop, I thought to myself. Please, go away, have mercy!

The clerk of the Court – a stern, serious-looking man dressed in a long black gown – got to his feet and addressed the judge. "Just for the record, your Honour, the date is Thursday 1st December 2005, and the time is 1p.m. The trial set before this court is between the music companies Arkace and Leobright Ltd., and Vicky Nolan the defendant."

The clerk stopped speaking, and a dramatic hush descended on the court. It was about to begin.

I looked up at the judge, resplendent in his wig, sitting enthroned behind an oak panelled lectern, the gold coloured royal crest imperious on the wall behind him. The whole thing was just so surreal; it was dizzying, like something out of a film, except there was no director to shout 'Cut'. This wasn't a film; this was real life; this was *my* life.

Judge Holden gave me a friendly smile. "Would you like a glass of water, Miss Nolan?"

"No, thank you, your Honour." I lifted a small bottle of Evian water I was clutching to show him I was OK.

The judge nodded before turning to speak to the plaintiff's barrister sitting below him. "Do carry on, Mr Hatter."

Mr Hatter, the barrister representing my ex-manager – that's right, my 'ex' manager, the guy who had promised to make me a star – rose to his feet. He was a tall, wormy character who spoke with a posh accent that didn't seem to match his appearance.

Removing an invisible speck of dust from his gown, he then went on to adjust his wig in a self-important manner. He glanced down for a second at his bundle of court papers – which were neatly tied with a claret-coloured ribbon – then frowning, he looked over at me in the dock, and flashed a wide cat-like smile, fixing me with an icy stare.

"I believe you've been to America, Vicky?" he asked. "California, is that correct?"

"Yes. To Los Angeles," I replied, trying to keep my voice level.

"Los Angeles!" he repeated, rather grandly. "Very nice, I'm sure. Please tell the court what it was like and what you were doing there." He smiled again briefly, though it was one of those smiles that didn't quite reach his eyes. "And take your time."

***

The Air Lingus A330 Airbus tipped its wing and banked to the right. Thirty-six thousand feet below, like an ocean frozen in mid tempest, the Colorado Rockies stretched into the far distance, their peaks – like white horses – capped with snow, mountain upon mountain.

I nudged Dad and we both gazed in awe at the breath-taking sight.

Suddenly, the captain's voice boomed over the intercom. "Ladies and gentlemen, I hope you're enjoying your flight to Los Angeles. The weather in LA is currently a warm and sunny 24 degrees."

My fellow passengers purred with delight; they were obviously as fed up as I was with Britain's cold November climate.

"And we have news just in about the US election," continued the captain. "After a recount in Florida, George W. Bush has been declared the winner and is still President of the United States."

Unlike the weather report, this piece of news was greeted with collective moans and groans throughout the cabin; the aircraft was seemingly full of Democratic John Kerry supporters – it was an Irish carrier, after all.

There was no news, however, that could bring me down – I was on my way to LA, and I felt great. I also felt like I looked the part; I'd got a fake tan especially for the trip, and while I smelled and looked like a Digestive biscuit, my pale complexion now had a much-needed Californian glow. As I looked out the window again, I couldn't help but grin in excitement. I was going to Hollywood!

As the stewardesses served dinner, Dad and I sat back in our wide, comfortable leather seats that reclined into beds at the flick of a switch. It was such a thrill flying transatlantic first class, which was something I never thought I would get to do. The cabin was a haven of spaciousness and luxury, our every whim and desire catered for.

There was champagne on boarding (although Dad and I opted for Diet Coke), little snacks and treats throughout the flight, and gourmet meals served on custom-made Waterford Crystal and Wedgewood china. There were no soggy sandwiches or over-stewed food to speak of... we ate chilli prawns tossed in garlic, fillet of steak and steamed vegetables, all followed by a pudding I couldn't pronounce the name of – you know something's top notch when you can't even say its name. I didn't even have to worry about the cost of everything; the entire trip was being paid for by my new friend and business associate, Jed Chankin.

After the meal, I surfed the TV channels, whiling away the hours watching the in-flight entertainment and listening to my tunes. It was a great flight.

A few hours later, the plane broke through a blanket of wispy cloud to begin its final descent. Now even more excited than ever, I settled back in my seat and once again looked out the window.

Viewed from the air, Los Angeles is an awesome sight; from horizon to horizon, the mega city is laid out in a grid-like pattern, the endless streets and boulevards merging as each borough connects seamlessly with its neighbour.

As the plane descended, tilting its wing tips in readiness for landing, the city was revealed in sharper detail: skyscrapers topped with pulsating strobe-lit towers, spaghetti-like freeways converging into chaotic loops before snaking off in all directions, their eight-lane highways encompassing apartment blocks, shops, and offices. Lower and lower, through the oval Plexiglas, I could see palm trees and gardens littered with swimming pools and basketball courts, parking lots, gas stations, and shopping malls, all basking under the Californian twilight. I couldn't wait to get out there.

At the end of our descent, we skimmed a humongous car park and then hit the tarmac with a thud, the loud roar of the engines pinning us to our seats. We had landed.

I smiled… OMG, I was in LA! I was really here!

Once we'd got off the plane, Dad and I walked through the airport and into the busy Check-In area. It was teeming with people queuing up at Passport Control (because of 9/11, the Americans were taking their security extremely seriously), and there was a lot going on: bag searches, dog sniffing, endless questioning… the whole atmosphere was very subdued, a big difference to the excitement I'd felt on the plane.

After what seemed like hours, we collected our luggage and finally made it into the Arrivals Hall. It was crammed with people greeting each other in loud LA accents, something that was like music to my ears.

I distinctly remember the day our family got Sky TV and I watched Nickelodeon for the first time. It made a big impact on me, and I instantly fell in love with the American pop-culture; the laid-back attitude, the casual fashion, the twangy dialects… I was moved to finally experience it for real.

Waiting to meet us at arrivals was Jed Chankin, or JC as he liked to be called – a long silver haired, fifty-something, larger than life character. He greeted me with the biggest smile I'd ever seen. He had an even louder voice than the people around him, and his energy was insatiable; he was like the Honey Monster who'd just eaten a large bag of Skittles. "Vicky! Great to see you! Welcome to LA!" he beamed.

Straight away I noticed the effect Jed had on people around us: he turned heads, his magnetic personality making him the constant centre of attention. On top of this, he was with his screenwriter friend Steve, who was filming my whole 'entrance' on a professional-looking camera, capturing my first steps on LA soil.

To be honest, it was a little overwhelming after an eleven-hour flight, and while I wasn't used to the superstar treatment at all, I tried my best to live up to Jed's expectations.

But that was nothing compared to what happened next: Whoosh! Exiting the terminal through a set of smoked glass sliding doors, we were bathed in a waft of humid Californian air – it was as though a giant hairdryer had been switched on and was pointing our way. All around us on the busy concourse, people were hailing taxis and jumping onto car rental coaches, heading off on the next step of their journey, whatever that may be.

I looked for our cab but it didn't seem to be there, and I was just about to ask Jed where it was when suddenly – and completely unbelievably – a gleaming dark-coloured stretch limo with blacked out windows glided to a halt in front of us.

I glanced behind me excitedly, wondering which celebrity was going to dash forward from the shadows and jump inside. Then the back door opened.

"OK," Jed said casually, "this is us."

I couldn't believe what I'd just heard, and going by the expression on my Dad's face, he couldn't either. Steve caught my reaction on camera, a sixteen-year-old schoolgirl arriving in LA, wearing UGGS and sporting a patchy-looking tan.

I didn't expect it at all, who was I? It was incredible, maybe this is how they do it here? It was a lot to take in.

Once we'd climbed inside the limo, the chauffer closed the door behind us with a muffled thud, the noise of the concourse immediately cutting to silence. The interior of the limo was huge – wall-to-wall leather seats, acres of legroom, a twinkling drinks cabinet, a neon starred ceiling, and Bose hi-fi.

I should have been revelling in the air-conditioned luxury of this amazing vehicle, but instead I felt a little uncomfortable and a bit intimidated, though I made a conscious effort not to show it, especially while there was a camera on me. In my head I was thinking, 'Jed's paid all this money for me to come all the way out here and work in the recording studio and meet his business associates. If he's gone to all this trouble, he must really believe in me'. So, I just hoped it would all be successful.

The trouble was, I still wasn't sure what success looked like. I mean, does anyone at 17 years old? – I mean, we're all winging it in our own way. It's a difficult thing, and any lack of self-confidence can be almost crippling.

However, as the limo pulled away and Jed began his witty banter I started to relax a little. He pulled open the drinks cabinet with a flourish. "Champagne? Bacardi? Wine? Bourbon? It's all at my fingertips"

You make an entrance like you've got it all

You've got a swagger and your walking tall

Yeah, I know your type

You're king of the night

But I've seen your name on the wall

Dad's not really much of a drinker, and as I didn't quite fancy knocking back a Bacardi, we plumped again for Diet Coke. To reciprocate Jed's amazing welcome, Dad delved into his hand luggage and produced a very expensive bottle of Remy Martin Louis XIII Cognac he'd bought at Manchester Airport at Jed's request. He said It was his favourite, and he was delighted. That set the tone nicely, and I started to relax even more.

Jed lived about fifteen miles from LAX Airport in a place just off Studio City, in a very cool neighbourhood set in the Hollywood

Hills. To get there we joined the 405 freeway and headed on through West Hollywood and over Mulholland Drive.

That's when it properly hit me: the in your face impact and glamour of LA – the sun-blistered highways, the tall tropical palm trees, the giant billboards featuring A-list celebrities promoting their latest TV and movie releases, everything three times the size of what we have in the UK. It was like driving through a futuristic dreamscape – a boy-racer computer game, even – the electric colours and pulsating pace giving everything an incredible vibe.

Place names flashed by – Century City, Beverly Hills, Bel Air. Then there were the houses; huge pastel-coloured mansions set behind lordly iron gates, laced with flowering bougainvillea and shaded by huge sculptured palm trees. It was just as dreamy as I'd imagined it, just as opulent, just as dazzling.

We drove into the Hollywood Hills towards Studio City, twisting and turning through lush green canyons of incredible beauty. At one point the roads became so steep and narrow that our stretch limo struggled to negotiate the hairpin bends. I stared out of the windows the entire time, trying to drink everything in.

Jed's friend Steve, kindly told me of some the history about Studio City, apparently It was named after a studio lot that was established in 1927 by the silent film producer Mack Sennett, famed for his slapstick Keystone Cops movies. Throughout the 40's, 50's and 60's, the area grew and began to attract artists, actors, and writers. They built hideaway homes in the hillsides and canyons, a perfect retreat for those wishing to escape the madness of Downtown LA while they worked on their artistic projects or relaxed in between film jobs.

I was delighted to find out that some famous A-listers were living in the same area as me: George Clooney, Ryan Gosling, and Miley Cyrus to name but a few. You never know, maybe I'd bump into one at Starbucks! It wasn't hard to see why they flocked to this place; the semi-tropical climate and stunning vistas, it was a no-brainer!

Halfway up a particularly steep hill the limo slowed to a crawl, before turning a sharp left and easing its massive bulk down a narrow driveway of semi-tropical scrub. Viewed from the front, Jed's house didn't look like much: a square box with art deco inspired entrance doors and the ubiquitous trash bins. But appearances can be deceiving, and the full grandeur of the place became evident round the back – nothing could have prepared me for its amazing TARDIS-like size and scale, I wondered, where was Dr Who?

Built into the hillside and with dizzying views of Coldwater Canyon, the house was a multi-layered, cutting-edge steel and glass design. Each level had its own deck, with each deck having its own hot tub and row of trendy sun loungers.

Jed couldn't wait to give us the guided tour, and he went from room to room like an excitable kid on Christmas morning, his arms waving all over the place as he pointed out the house's unique features – dazzling white walls, sumptuous charcoal-coloured carpets, Italian floor tiles, and marble bathrooms with Trump-like gold taps.

We trooped up and down the many staircases like prospective home buyers, ooh-ing and ahh-ing at every room, breathing in the aroma of perfumed sandalwood. The thing that struck me most was the amount of light flooding in through the enormous floor to ceiling windows; sunlight bounced and reflected off the chic contemporary furnishings from all angles, giving the place a real sparkle and energy about it.

To someone like me, who was brought up in a Victorian house in northwest England – a region famed for its dull, cloud spoiling light – this was a revelation; it lifted my spirits.

You couldn't fail to be motivated in a place like this Mr Hatter, and that's exactly why Jed had brought me to California: to be motivated and hopefully to create.

Mr Hatter, the slippery-faced barrister, looked up from his notes and faced the court "Please tell the court exactly what you mean, Vicky, by the words 'to create', I mean, I want to ask you the question, have you guessed the riddle yet? Because I haven't."

Glimpses of Me… Lipstick, Heels and Songwriting

Another day, another makeup counter. I'm wearing a full face of makeup and stood in high heels at the cosmetic counter at Selfridges – no sales and no customers – it's very quiet.

Luckily, when it's quiet my creative juices get flowing, I use my downtime to write lyric ideas and song themes on paper till roll from the cash register.

"Hmm… 'Your Ghost' is a cool song title." I scribble a few lines for a chorus and then a verse. I like the idea. I stuff the till receipt in my pocket for safekeeping.

You have to take inspiration from wherever you can find it.

6

Canyons and melodies

I woke up the next morning, bleary eyed and with a runny nose, and for a brief second, I had no idea where I was. Sharp daggers of sunlight pierced the shuttered window while traffic faintly rumbled in the distance.

Then I remembered: I was in LA! The City of Angels! Smiling excitedly, I leapt out of bed and flung open the window: sapphire sky! Lush green hillside! A view so intense and beautiful, anything seemed possible. I wished I could wake up like this every morning.

I joined Dad and Jed for breakfast on the balcony that extended out from the kitchen, seemingly floating in mid-air. We were hovering above the valley floor, while the birds and hawks were wheeling in the heavens. Poynton, it was not.

Jed asked me how I'd slept, but as he talked he kept glancing up at the jagged silhouettes of the freewheeling kites and hawks. "Those Goddam birds!" he shouted. "They frighten the hell out of my cats."

Damn birds? Damn cats! My allergies were back!! I'd covered the bed the night before with some of my clean clothes to try and limit my contact with the cat fluff on the bed sheets from Jed's beloved cats, but to no avail, the cat fluff had won! I had a runny nose all round! I decided however, to keep the peace, I'd keep my allergy to myself, and I continued to listen to Jed as he ran through the coming day's schedule.

After a few minutes, he glanced at his vintage Omega watch.

"Some of the guys are coming over later; Arron and Karma, really talented session musicians and writers. They've heard you sing and can't wait to work with you," he explained. "I've set up an improvised studio in the lounge and pool areas; I'm sure it'll just be great there."

It was clear that Jed was going out of his way to make me feel at home, something I really appreciated. It was still daunting though being in a new place, with new people who all had such high expectations of me, but Jed was making it easier.

After breakfast, we made our way into the makeshift studio, which included anything we could possibly need: mics, headphones, sound booth, a small digital mixing desk, computers, guitars, and a keyboard. It was a bright, sunlit room with peaceful views over the valley, the perfect stimulus for song writing. Tucked away in the corner was a pool table, a mad sound system complete with acres of CD's and vinyl, and the coolest custom-made bar. I could definitely get used to this. Cheers Jed!

The doorbell chimed, and Jed went out into the atrium and hallway, reappearing seconds later with two hip-looking guys in their late twenties. Both had shaved heads and wore baggy cargo pants, caps and sweatshirts. They were typical music junkies, their eyes lighting up when they saw all the recording equipment, and they wasted no time scrutinising the components in front of them.

Jed made the introductions. "Vicky, this is Arron and Karma. The two talented guys I told you about."

I gave them both a hug and then we all sat down while Jed went off to the chiller to collect fresh waters. They asked me about the flight and how I was enjoying LA so far, I told them I loved it.

Those first brief moments together with new writing partners are so important; you know very quickly if you're going to get on, and more importantly, if there's any creative spark between you. Without that, there's not much point in plugging anything in, but from the word go I knew I'd get on with Arron and Karma. They were chatty, relatable, and they totally got my English sense of droll humour. Luckily, I got theirs too. We were making a connection.

On the surface, you'd expect them both to be exclusively into rap and hip-hop, but I was pleased to learn that they were massively inspired by soul. Arron and Karma were fascinated by my northern English accent and sense of daft irony, it was a good laugh all round, but as soon as Jed came back into the room they both became quieter and more cautious. Jed's character was loud and dominant, and it had an effect on everybody. That's the thing about JC: however friendly and helpful he may appear, he's still the boss, he's still the head honcho, and he lets everyone know it.

You can say I'm normal way too formal

You can say I'm out of here

You can call me boring sat there yawning

Maybe you should drink more beer

All three of us got down to work right away, Arron, Karma, and I swapping melodies, hooks, and verses like we'd been composing together for years. It all seemed very natural – a walk in the park.

There I was, a sixth former schoolgirl who'd bunked off school and ran away to a fabulous house in the Hollywood Hills, taking my chances, and going for it. I soaked up every moment I could whilst at the same time trying to breathe through my allergy-ridden sinuses.

Arron and Karma were both so welcoming of my ideas and input and were genuinely complimentary of me, although at this point I still didn't feel like I could call myself a singer songwriter. Even though I had been writing songs for a few years, in order to call myself a songwriter I had to believe I was actually good at it. I knew my belief would eventually come with time, however, it was all about growing more confident with experience. And I was certainly getting a lot of experience.

During the morning and late into the afternoon, a steady stream of visitors arrived – a vice president here, a producer there

– all keen to check me out, to see for themselves Jed's new 'discovery'. To entertain his guests, Jed had plates of nibbles and drinks brought in, and many trips to Ralphs and Panera Bread were made down on Ventura Boulevard for food to keep us all in the swing. The atmosphere was chilled, and the conversation centred around LA gossip and music chit-chat – who's signing with who, which executive was on the up, and whose career was going down the pan. A lot of it was way over my head. People played pool, drank beer, and smoked cigarettes on the balconies. At least I think they were cigarettes… It was all very fun and relaxed, very LA.

Then, towards late afternoon, in walked Jed's business associate Tom, a big bear of a man sporting a Cali-tan and a huge bushy moustache that completely enveloped his top lip. He wore a colourful surfer shirt that billowed from his waist. He reminded me of a chubby Frank Zappa, though his hair was shorter. As soon as he entered the room everyone stared at him, acknowledging his presence – you couldn't really miss him. Marching straight over to me he beamed, "Vicky! You're finally here! Welcome to LA!"

We embraced, and I told him how happy I was to meet him, which was the truth: I was face-to-face with Tom Ross, a new contact and associate, a very senior music executive and one of the founders of the music division of the famed talent agency CAA, no less! He really knew his stuff and he was going to help me.

Pleasantries over, I went back to the recording session, while Tom took a seat and listened in. Having such a powerful, influential man in the room fired me up, and I raised my game, hitting each note with smoothness and clarity, really reaching for and finding the emotion in the songs.

When I was finished he stood up and applauded enthusiastically. He beckoned me over, lent towards me and said, in a sage like way, "Wow, you certainly have some pipes on you for one so small and young. All you need now is to live life a little and write some great songs." He smiled. "In the end, it's all about the songs" I thought, maybe I'd write a great song one day.

INT.   JEWELLERY   BOUTIQUE   SHOP.   WEST

HOLLYWOOD. DAYTIME. SUNNY.

VICKY and JED go into a jewellery shop and look at jewellery and watches at the counter. Jed calls over to the shop assistant.

                    JED
 Hi... can we look at those bracelets.

               SHOP ASSISTANT
     Of course, Sir, glad to...

SHOP ASSISTANT reaches for the bracelets and puts them on top of the counter. JED picks a gold daisy chain bracelet from the tray and puts it on VICKY'S wrist.

                    JED
    Yeah... that looks great sweetie!

                   VICKY
      It does, it's really nice...

JED beckons over the shop assistant.

                    JED
            We'll take it!
VICKY looks surprised!
                   VICKY

NO! Jed... I couldn't, really no... it's too

expensive.

                    JED
Don't be silly sweetie, JC wants you to
                 have it.

              SHOP ASSISTANT
Would you like me to gift wrap it for you
                  Sir?

                   VICKY
           No, Jed... really...

JED ignores VICKY and says to the SHOP
ASSISTANT

                    JED
  No, that's ok, we'll take it... she's
               wearing it

VICKY looks embarrassingly at the shop
assistant as she takes the bracelet to the
till, then smiles awkwardly at JED

                   VICKY
              Thanks JED

                              CUT TO :

The early morning sun beat down as I power-walked through the rolling canyons overlooking Studio City, the sweet smell of pine, oak, and primrose hanging in the air. All along the narrow, twisting road, wild flowers dotted the grass verge like little buds of neon.

Reaching the corner of a gorse-covered bend, I stopped to take in the view: far below, the San Fernando Valley smouldered in the gathering heat, and scanning the hazy metropolis, my eyes came to rest on the snow-capped San Gabriel Mountains, their jagged outlines rising in the far distance like the teeth of a saw blade dipped in icing sugar. It was truly stunning. Another clear, bright, California day. Do clouds live here? I wondered. Or do they only exist in the UK?

Every morning since arriving here, I had taken this same route: turn left out of Jed's house and follow the winding road for a mile or two. I wasn't the only one, either – countless super-fit LA joggers and walkers would pass me, MP3 players glued to their ears, an incessant tinny beat following in their wake. From my vantage point above the gorge, I watched as they zigzagged down the canyon before disappearing into palm-shaded entrance gates, where no doubt a refreshing breakfast of sliced mango and blueberries awaited them on the terrace. Heaven!

At this moment, however, it was just me and the chirping crickets.

Suddenly, my Blackberry pinged. I reached into my bag, grabbed my phone, and finding the cool shade of a pine tree, I sat down on the warm orange dirt.

I had two emails, and opening the first, I saw it was from my younger sister Harriet, sent the previous day: *Hi Vic! Crap weather here. Rain, rain, and rain. Hope it's better where you are. Just got home from school. Yuck! Taking Heidi for a walk now before tea. Love you. Haz x. PS. Mum sends her love x*

Aww, I miss home, I thought.

I opened the second email to find it was from Brian, my lawyer representing me in court, defending me in my messy legal dispute with my ex-manager William: *Hi Vicky. Hope you're having a good trip.*

Some bad news I'm afraid, I'm back in court today; another case management conference, it didn't go as planned, but don't worry. I'll give you an update later how it went. Speak soon, Brian (cc Kevin)

In an instant, a feeling of dread swept over me. It was a message I didn't want to see, a reminder of the bad side of the music industry I was trying to forget while I was out here having fun. I just wanted the whole thing to go away.

Cursing modern technology for invading my California dreamin', I thought to myself, 'This is crazy! My lawyers told me I could end my contracts, they said I was entitled to do so, and if I did, that would be it' – end of! No breach of contract.

Just then, Brian's voice popped into my head: "The contracts aren't fair, Vicky. They're odious, the court will see that, don't worry"

But I am WORRYING BRIAN!

I just didn't understand any of it anymore, things were getting way out of control, and it was all way above my head.

So put me in a headlock
Race me 'til my heart stops
You can only break my bones
Hit me with a full stop
All you've got is sticks and stones.

I got up slowly, dusting the pine needles from my tracksuit bottoms. The beauty surrounding me had vanished in an instant, a thousand thoughts and concerns swirling in my head.

I trudged back uphill to the house, worried about how all this was affecting my mum and younger sisters. Then there was my Dad to consider: how the hell was he coping with all this? He'd spent most of the flight out here trawling through thick files of legal case notes that he'd brought with him, most of which neither I nor he could fully understand.

Deep down, I think he knew he was out of his depth, but it

was his fighting spirit that pushed him to make sense of this unnecessary, messy-as-hell situation. He was protecting his family, like he always did.

As I walked down the canyon, I looked up and saw a pair of kites circling on the breeze, hovering above me like vultures. They obviously knew something I didn't – a bad omen!

When I got back I took a quick shower, which didn't help to unblock my nose at all – pesky cats! Passing me on the stairs, Jed barked, "Meeting on the patio in five, Vicky! I wanna discuss plans for the day."

"Yes, JC," I replied, trying not to sound too intimidated.

I jumped to it. Dad was already in the kitchen grinding coffee beans when I got downstairs (he's addicted to fresh coffee) and I told him about the email from Brian.

A concerned look flashed across his face, though he hid it expertly behind a smile of mock bravado. "I'll sort it, Vicky, don't worry" he said casually. I could tell this legal thing was stressing him out, though he didn't want to show it. He was being strong as always, but I could see the faint cracks starting to appear through his calm demeanour – even from behind his shades.

I grabbed some bottled water from the fridge and then we wandered out onto the deck. The morning traffic making its noise below down to Ventura; Los Angeles was gearing itself up for another congested day. We sat at a stylish glass topped table, burning hot in the strong sunlight, a marble ashtray at its centre, overflowing with Jed's cigarette butts from the previous night.

Talk of the devil.

"Right guys!" The man himself bounded onto the patio wearing tortoiseshell shades and a garish Hawaiian shirt. "Busy morning. Need to make some calls." He took a seat and threw Dad a set of car keys. "Be a bud and drive into Studio City for me, would ya? We're getting low on supplies. Ralph's supermarket is at the bottom of the hill; you can't miss it. While you're there swing by the bank – Wells Fargo, on Ventura – and deposit this." He handed my Dad an envelope. "By the way, I've had the car tweaked a little, so be careful on the gas… it's a sleeper."

"A sleeper?" asked Dad, confused.

"Yeah." An impish grin lit up Jed's face. "It goes like a rocket."

As the days went by, I was learning more and more about JC. He was so unorthodox and off-the-wall; one minute he was smothering you with charm, and the next he was ordering you to go shopping. Maybe it was his kooky Californian way – open and generous in spirit, but always prepared to test the system and push personal relationships to the limit.

As kooky as he was, I really felt I could learn something from him; he had such an engaging way with people – whether you were just an ordinary shop assistant or a powerful president or executive, he treated everybody the same. He was a smooth operator and knew how to work people, which was totally new to me. When you're just starting out, you think you know all the answers to get ahead, and I really believed there was a secret formula to success that I had to know about in order to win at life. I think I know now that part of that formula is all about the sweet talk, the blag if you will. Confidence and conviction is what sees you through, plus blag, and more blag – everybody everywhere is secretly blagging it, and Jed was great at it.

Leaving the house, Dad buzzed open the garage door, flooding the interior with sunlight as the smell of petrol and car wax rose to meet us. I didn't know what he'd been expecting – a Ferrari or something, probably – but his face dropped when he clapped eyes on the little Toyota MR2 parked in the corner: a low, squat two-seater, with retro Cali plates emblazoned with the strap line 'The Golden State'.

He gave the car the once over. "Strange," he said, "it looks like a bog-standard model to me, but the wheels are non-spec. Look, they're slick racing wheels."

I had no idea what he meant, but I soon found out – as did Dad.

Inside, the car was a complete tip; the floor, seats, and dashboard were littered with empty water bottles and candy wrappers, the ashtray overflowing with cigarette butts. The stale scent of Jed's cologne mixed with air freshener hit us square between the eyes, and the first thing we did was open the sunroof and windows to let some air in.

Dad started the engine and gave it a rev, the smell of premium unleaded polluting the garage. "Sounds promising," he said, though his expression said otherwise.

Having never driven in LA before, he took a deep breath before setting off, and soon we were creeping cautiously off the drive and out onto the dusty hillside. Now, this is a man who mostly drives a white van at a crawling pace of only 28mph. My bum cheeks were clenched with nerves as we got out onto the road.

He feathered the accelerator nervously, the souped-up engine growling like a caged tiger as we descended into the valley, twisting and turning past peach coloured houses with terracotta roofs half concealed behind a mass of semi-tropical greenery – the occasional glimpse of Mexican gardeners working between the gaps in the trees.

Kicking up a shower of stones and dust, we finally made it to the bottom, where we turned right onto Coldwater. The road was jammed with the morning commuter traffic from over the hill, but at the first flat stretch we came to, Dad hit the accelerator. The little MR2 responded instantly, shooting forward and pinning us to our seats.

Dad laughed like a naughty schoolboy. "I can see why Jed had those tyres put on! It's nippy as hell!"

We turned right onto Ventura, a five-lane boulevard lined with tall palm trees, and the heart of Studio City. Banks, delis, strip malls, and fast food outlets flashed by, a commercial kaleidoscope shimmering beneath the California sun. The place had a kind of retro feel about it. Dad said, it reminded him of the cartoon show the Flintstones - maybe it was the bowling alley.

Turning right, we pulled into Ralph's, a cream-coloured supermarket set back from the road. Dad grabbed a trolley while

I checked my Blackberry – I was like a moth to a flame. There were, however, no messages from my lawyer Brian: relief!

Whilst Dad eyed up the fried chicken counter, I saw Ashlee Simpson at the salad bar: my first celeb sighting! I was chuffed, and I couldn't wait to pass on the juicy gossip to my friends when I got home.

After shopping at Ralph's, we headed back down Ventura and called in at Wells Fargo bank, its name evoking fond memories for me of watching old American movies. It reminded me so much of the Wild West, I half expected Jesse James to burst in with his six-shooter to rob the place.

It was an interesting shopping trip, some time on my own, and for now, at least, life was a breeze.

Glimpses of Me... Just Walking the Dog

"Come on, Frankie! Let's go for a walk!"

My eight-year-old German Shepherd (who despite her age, still looks like a puppy) knows exactly what I mean, and her tail thrums with excitement when she hears those words. She licks my face as I bend down to attach the lead; it's hard to pin her down as she turns and spins around, loop-de-loop, all excited. "Stop it, Frankie!"

That's the thing about dogs – when you love them, they shower you with unconditional love back.

Coat, gloves, keys. Check. It's cold outside – a snowy winter's morning – Snowflakes falling like goose feathers from the sky – the landscape covered in a white blanket of slush! Chill!

I open the five-bar gate at the side of the house and step into the farmer's field, my wellies instantly sinking into the soft sodden earth.

I scan the field and let her off the lead. She can't wait, she's off! her sable coloured coat moving in sharp contrast to the blinding white snow.

I watch as she disappears through the snowy curtain, listening as her bark faintly recedes to the farthest corner of the field. Oh No! Sheep!! "Frankie! Frankie! Come baaaack!!"

7

Give me the chorus baby!

It was nonstop at Jed's. He was clearly keen to impress me, introducing me to all his friends and confidants, and the next morning he told me that he'd arranged a photo shoot with Maurice Rinaldi, one of LA's top photographers. I didn't know who he was, but I was really looking forward to meeting him, and while the shoot was booked for the following day, Jed wanted Dad and I to meet Maurice and his wife Lillian beforehand.

So, after a busy morning spent song writing, we drove over to his house in Studio City, parking on a quiet residential street that resembled the set of Desperate Housewives – we were surrounded by pastel-coloured timber fronted houses, white picket fences, and neatly trimmed lawns boarded by twee flower beds, each with its own front porch festooned with hanging baskets. It really did look like the folksy American dream. Maurice's house was just as cute, with small Tudor style dormer windows and timbers painted in soft blues and greens.

We squeezed onto the drive, which was full of vintage Mercedes Benz cars parked higgledy-piggledy, some pristine, others dilapidated and in need of some TLC.

As we approached, the front door opened with a flourish and Maurice stepped out onto the porch to greet us. Dressed in loose fitting cotton trousers and a colourful open neck shirt, he was a tall, slim man in his mid-sixties, with long, steel grey hair and a salt and pepper beard that gave him the look of a trendy Steven Spielberg.

"Great to meet you, Vicky! Wow!" he said, with a conspicuous Aussie twang.

After a quick Google, I'd found out that his photographs had graced the front covers of *Vogue* and *Playboy*, and he was excited about meeting *me*?! Really?

He was gregarious and a bit of a showman (maybe it's hard-wired into celebrity photographers, like part of their DNA), and like most Californians, he came from a mishmash of different cultures and backgrounds (while born in Italy, he was of Australian descent). Before taking us into the house, he was keen to show us his collection of vintage Mercedes.

"They're my passion," he drawled. "I search the world looking for bargains, buy them, then import them. It's a hobby of mine, though a damned expensive one. Look at the shape of these babies, the way they're constructed – like works of art," he said proudly.

After admiring his cars, Maurice led us into the house. It was furnished in a rustic, shabby-chic style, with natural pine furniture and vases of fresh flowers dotted here and there to add a splash of colour to the cool, Scandinavian decor.

We soon discovered the source behind this design – Maurice's glamorous Norwegian wife, Lillian Müller, an ex-Playboy centrefold, health guru, and celebrity actress. She floated into the room wearing skin-tight denim jeans and a figure-hugging sweater. Although she was in her early fifties, she had the body and face of a woman half her age, with long, strawberry blonde hair and sparkling blue eyes. She was beautiful.

She took us into the kitchen to make some tea, and as the kettle boiled on the stove, I asked about her career.

"I started modelling in Norway," she explained. "Then I moved to London, where I did Page Three a couple of times. I got spotted by Hugh Heffner; you know, the guy who owns *Playboy*. Hugh's turned out to be a good friend. Anyway, I was asked to do the centrefold, and from there I was voted Playmate of the Month, then Playmate of the Year." She said all this in a completely matter-of-fact manner, as if she was telling me about her job down at the bank.

Bringing the tea over, she continued, "Shortly after, I got into films and TV. I appeared in *Remington Steele*, *Starsky and Hutch*, *Magnum. PI*, *Charlie's Angels*, you name it. It was a blast. I even appeared in the Rod Stewart video, *Do Ya think I'm Sexy?* Remember that?"

"*I* do!!" exclaimed Dad, a little too excitedly, I thought.

Being an expert in such matters, and noticing that Dad was obviously a fan, Lillian sashayed across the kitchen, opened a drawer, and presented him with her latest calendar: 'Lillian Müller at 50'.

"Ta, Lillian! That's lovely," Dad replied, having a quick flick through. I tried not to laugh as his eyes widened by the second – let's just say the pictures were on the more glamorous side, with Lillian wearing bikini bottoms that resembled dental floss more than anything else.

I changed the subject, and quickly too. "You look so young!" I cried. "What's your secret?"

"Well, Vicky, like most things in life, it's down to hard work and dedication. I only consume natural products – water, no alcohol, and so on – and I follow a strict vegetarian diet. I exercise daily and get plenty of sleep."

I thought that it sounded like a lot of work, but it was definitely working for her, as the expression on my dad's face confirmed.

Jed then presented Maurice with a gift – the expensive brandy dad had picked up at Manchester Airport Duty Free. Maurice was thrilled, and I couldn't help but laugh; Jed was working his magic again!

***

The next day, Jed, Steve the cameraman, and I jumped into a limo and headed back to Maurice's house. Steve was there to document the day, filming the shoot from start to finish, and while I was getting used to his presence a little more now, it still seemed a little weird, to say the least.

When we arrived, Maurice took us round the back of the house towards his studio, which was nestled at the far end of a dense, tropical garden. It was like walking through a mini paradise, with clumps of palms, exotic-looking plants, and little golden birds flitting in and out of the sun-dappled shade. Yet again, I couldn't help but think it was a far cry from home.

My senses were stirred as we followed a stone path that curved past a kidney-shaped swimming pool, its turquoise water shimmering with echoes of light, like a Hockney painting. As we rounded a bend edged with ornamental grasses and succulent Aloe Vera, the path narrowed before broadening out and revealing Maurice's hidden gem of a studio.

Tucked inside the entrance door was a tinted glass panel with the initials MR emblazoned across it in gold, and the light-hearted Maurice from the day before now changed as he led us inside. We were there to work; it was time to get serious.

"Come and meet the make-up artist," he said, leading me into a side room that featured wall-to-wall racks of clothes.

Standing behind a table that was covered with the tools of her trade – mascaras, eye shadows, sponges, brushes, lipsticks, and more – was a woman in her mid-forties, dressed all in black. She had long, Titian-red hair and she wore dark rimmed glasses. She was very striking.

"Vicky, this is Mary Resnik," said Maurice. "She's one of the top make-up artists in Hollywood. She's worked on all the stars."

"HI, Vicky. Great to meet you," said Mary politely. "Take a seat in front of the mirror"

As Maurice left the room to prepare for the shoot, I sat down tentatively in a swivel chair in front of Mary. I had great make-up expectations – I was about to be 'worked on' by a lady whose magical hands had caressed and cajoled the faces of countless A-listers!

Again, I started to feel a bit unsure and out of my depth, but I needn't have worried; Mary put me at ease straight away, asking me questions about my life in England and what I hoped to achieve out here. I told her a little about myself, and as she began to apply the blusher and eyeliner, I plucked up the courage to quiz her about her famous clientele. Just as matter-of-factly as Lillian had been, she ran through a list of stellar names too numerous to mention, though the one that stuck in my mind was Michael Jackson... *THE* MICHAEL JACKSON! Now that's cool!

With my make-up applied, I got changed into a black cami top and a short, gypsy type skirt slashed with pink mesh. I styled myself for the shoot, something you think would be fun but in reality, it's quite stressful. I was pretty convinced that the clothes I'd chosen for the day would make me look like the 'pop star' they wanted me to be, whilst still staying true to myself. It was a difficult combination to achieve, but I thought I'd pulled it off.

Maurice's voice boomed from the next room. "OK, superstar! Ready when you are!"

In response, I jokingly bit my fist, as if I was worried. "Don't worry, honey," purred Mary reassuringly. "You'll be fine; Maurice is a pussycat."

Hoping that was true, I let Mary accompany me into the studio where Maurice was waiting, Nikon-in-hand, along with Jed and Steve, who was still filming the whole thing.

There was a raised platform surrounded by lights and diffusers in the corner of the room, with power cables running everywhere. The backdrop was a neutral grey.

Still nervous, I stepped onto the platform, and straight away I could feel the fierce heat from the studio lights – cooled somewhat by a swivelling electric fan, but intense nonetheless.

Jed walked over and adjusted my hair. "Relax, superstar, you'll be just fine." Stepping down, he pointed at the camera. "Ok, Vicky. Gimmie natural. Natural and sexy."

I smiled, tilting my head this way and that while Maurice fired off a volley of shots. I was still nervous, and it felt really awkward. The first few shots of any shoot always feel awkward, though, and

I knew that I'd soon ease into it. After all, I'd spent my whole life posing in front of mirrors at home; this was just the same, I told myself.

Crouching and prowling, Maurice shouted encouragement while he took the shots: "Hey! Hey!... Look at me, kiddo! Yeah, do it, move your hands too, your hair... Whoo!... Looking good!... It's all there (pointing to his eyes) … your eyes, your eyes! If it ain't workin' there, it ain't workin' anywhere!"

I couldn't help but laugh – he reminded me of an Australian Austin Powers; he may as well have been yelling, "Yeeeesss baby, looking good… Miaow!"

Unlike some photographers I'd worked with in the past, Maurice brought out the best in me. His sense of humour soon made me forget how famous he was, and after the initial awkwardness, I began to relax and really enjoy the shoot.

I did a series of costume changes – slashed denim jeans and a tight kimono, a silk blouse, baggy black pants, and a crop-top. For the next few hours, I posed my arse off. Sounds glamorous, doesn't it? But it really was very hard work. For hours I pouted, preened, and posed, even though I was tired and starting to flag.

After a short break and a quick tease of the hair from Mary, I changed into faded jeans and a white T-shirt with leopard boots; a sort of Shania Twain, girl-next-door look. Maurice led me out of the studio and posed me on a set of stone steps, where we started the whole routine again.

By the time the shoot was over, I was knackered, utterly exhausted. I'd also had the best day ever.

As we waited for the limo to take me back to Jed's, Maurice walked over and said, "You're a natural, kiddo. The camera loves ya."

I smiled happily; coming from him, it made me feel like I was doing something right, and it was the ultimate compliment.

We all jumped in the limo to head back to base, and as we drove through Studio City, the driver buzzed down the privacy glass and asked us if we wanted some music on.

"Hell yeah!" shouted Jed, opening the glass door of the in-car chiller. We helped ourselves to Diet Coke and lots of ice, even though the air-con was switched to the max, it was warm, and it had been a hot day. Then the music kicked in through the speakers – *Girls on Film* by Duran Duran. I was pretty sure Jed had cued that up for me especially.

As we headed down Ventura Boulevard, I thought to myself, 'This must be what it's all about – glamour and the excitement. Wow… I was living the dream, in the place of dreams, and I couldn't be happier.

Suddenly, my Blackberry vibrated in my pocket, and even before I looked at it I could feel my good vibe starting to melt as fast as the ice in my drink. As I glanced at the screen, my suspicions were confirmed: it was an email from Brain, my lawyer back in the UK. I opened the inbox with my eyes half shut and squinted to see the words; *please call me ASAP*.

In an instant, the magic of the day had completely disappeared, the excitement had gone and my Diet Coke had gone flat.

Glimpses of Me…. Face in The Mirror

I plod into the bathroom and switch on the light. It's early. I've hardly slept. My face has been driving me crazy all night, disturbing my sleep – my skin, itchy and sore. I bet it's back.

Building up the courage, I dare to look in the mirror to see the damage.

Oh no! There they are again – big red rashes covering my eyes and forehead. Even without my contact lenses in I can see it: that horrible flare-up on my face and neck. I look horrible! My face – my poor, oozy, flaky face. My eczema!! It's back like a curse.

Normally I don't let it bother me. Sometimes people stare, while others point out 'helpfully' to me that I have a rash – yes, I know I do, thank you very much!

Is it something I've touched? Let me think… have I been near any animals? Maybe it's something I've eaten? It's so FRUSTRATING!!!! It's like a puzzle with no clues.

Right, time for makeup. Cosmetics – a girl's best friend. A few expert dabs here and there, and some bright lipstick to distract from the rashes.

Yes, that'll do it; now I can face the world.

FADE IN :

INT. VICKY'S LAWYER'S HOUSE. DINING ROOM.
EVENING.

VICKY is sitting around the dining room
table with her lawyer at his home - BRIAN
a man in his fifties. The atmosphere is
cordial. They're waiting for VICKYS
barrister AMANDA MICHALES to arrive for the
meeting.

AMANDA, a professional lady in her
thirties, enters the room confidently. She
walks over to VICKY with an outstretched
hand.

                    AMANDA
Hello, Vicky. It's a pleasure to meet you.
  I'm Amanda. Amanda Michaels....your new
            barrister. I'm very much
   looking forward to representing you in
                    court.

AMANDA and VICKY shake hands. AMANDA puts
her briefcase on the table and takes off
her coat.

                    BRIAN
  How was the journey up Amanda... good?

AMANDA

Yes, no problems thank you... all good.

AMANDA takes a seat at the dining table, opens her briefcase and puts her legal papers across the table.

AMANDA

Oh, Brian. Is there any chance we may have some tea please?

BRIAN

Of course, Amanda, tea, no problem... on Its way.

BRIAN rises and leaves the room. AMANDA shuffles her notes and looks across the table towards VICKY

AMANDA

(*smiles confidently*)
Right, Vicky. We're here to win... yes?

VICKY

Yes... definitely, we need to win!

8

Stay composed, and just ad lib…

Leaving Hollywood's hustle and bustle – the screaming billboards, the studio lots, the fast food joints, the designer outlets stalked by fashionistas – we made our way to the 101 Freeway, heading west through Sherman Oaks and Encino before exiting at the Valley Circle intersection.

As the traffic thinned, the terrain changed from the LA urban landscape to parched desert scrub; suddenly, all was peace and tranquillity. Continuing along the road in the dry heat, we drove north through Valley Circle into the pretty suburb of Hidden Hills – a small pocket of calm resting on the outskirts of the city.

The roads and streets were quiet, the broad sidewalks strangely oversized and empty, devoid of people. Nobody seems to walk around here, I thought - nothing like the tiny, winding streets at home. We cruised past mile upon mile of spacious, large houses, painted in a myriad of sun-faded colours, beautiful shrubs and palms everywhere. On and on we drove... nobody in, nobody around – even the gardeners were absent – It was a little eerie.

All this space was wasted on me. Where were all the locals? Where was the activity? The hubbub? Maybe it was just an English thing – coming from a small crowded island, I was used to seeing people milling about on the streets, always something going on, with hustle and bustle on every corner.

Here, it was sunny, hazy, and calm, a big landscape and a big sky. Whenever we passed houses, it was like something out of a film – perfectly manicured lawns with rows and rows of white picket fences just like in *The Truman Show*. Maybe things swung into life in the evening, I thought to myself, after the Angelinos had battled the busy commute home, making it back across the San Fernando Valley to their silent empty homes – yes, maybe the place was alive then. It was so different to my own home, but I loved it – the whole place just fascinated me.

Eventually, we turned onto Drew's road. Drew was the new producer Jed had set me up with; a mega talented guy by all accounts – guitar, piano, drums, he played the lot. I felt slightly uneasy as we made our way along the road; our working relationship hadn't been quite worked out yet or made clear, and I didn't really know what the plan was for the session. Even though I trusted Jed and his dealings, I always like to know and be clear on where I stand; I hate letting people down and not fulfilling their expectations, and I didn't want that to happen here.

Dad parked the rental car alongside a fire hydrant on the sidewalk. The road itself was on a steep incline, so when I clambered out and stepped onto the high kerb, I felt even smaller than I actually was.

Reaching back into the car for my bottle of water – which was now warm and not at all refreshing – I took a swig whilst scanning the horizon. It looked like the landscapes in the old Cowboy and Indian films, where tomahawk-wielding Apache Indians would descend from the hills in a big cloud of dust, ready to ambush the cavalry. No, the hills in the Hidden Hills were not hidden at all!

Walking up Drew's curved driveway, I felt a tingle of nerves – 17-year-old nerves – and what felt like a butterfly swirling around in my stomach.

This was a new test for me: a music collaboration with an LA producer recommended by Tom Ross. I'd written with a handful of writers/producers already – some more professional and experienced than others – but this was different, something very cool. Another lucky American experience.

Although I was feeling a little daunted by the whole thing, at the same time I felt quietly confident in my writing ability, and as I knew by now, confidence is everything. It gives you the power to be yourself and work with conviction and belief. It's true, experience helps you grow. Still, I like to treat each session as though it's my first; in my head, I'm only as good as my last song.

We ducked under an arbour blossoming with flowers and walked through into the back garden. The studio was situated next to a rock-themed swimming pool that was surrounded by children's slides and swings. The guy was obviously a family man – my cautious mood eased down a notch.

Drew greeted us with an easy-going smile before leading us inside to meet his lovely family. I was relaxed and put at ease by his warm, friendly way; some producers can be all mystery and ego – which can be a little off-putting – but Drew was nothing like this, he was down-to-earth and full of interesting conversation.

He took us into a chill-out room off the main studio, pulling some iced water from the refrigerator (there's always iced water in music studios) and making me feel right at home. We chatted for ages, getting to know one another's musical likes and dislikes, and discussing different song themes and subjects that I wanted to write about. Even though I had a boyfriend at the time, I was determined not to harp on about love and heartache all the time, like many other singers my age did. Heartbreak wasn't something I'd been through (not by that point, anyway) so I didn't want to appear naive or vulnerable. I was all about Girl Power – what can I say? The Spice Girls' motto on feminism made a big impact on me, as it did to many other girls my age, and I wanted to add that feeling, that message, into my music.

At the time, I was in the middle of a messy court case, and it felt appropriate to sing about things relevant to me. I never really went through a rebellious phase in my teens, so this was my first chance to stick two fingers up to all the bad stuff that was going on around me, stuff that made me angry. Grrr... Take that, world! This was going to be my anthem to get me through this difficult time, an anthem that would hopefully speak to thousands of other girls like me!

So now we had a theme, and a title for the song: *'Over You'*. I sat on a sofa in the studio and poured all of my frustration into the lyrics, all my fury and my irritation. It felt good to write – it was a real cathartic exercise – and even better to sing it. It was liberating because it was the truth, *my* truth.

I'd been through this legal limbo for what seemed like forever – all the bull-crap, all the lies and the promises. My family and I were affected all because of someone's bruised ego, and even though I knew deep down that I hadn't, I hated feeling like I'd failed everyone. That kind of feeling is awful – it saps all of your strength and fuels your bad dreams. In some ways, the court case was becoming a real education: life sometimes throws you curveballs and things don't always go the way you planned, and even though I was being tested, I knew that I would eventually come out on the other side, hopefully, stronger and more experienced.

So, we had the lyrics, and now we needed a 'sound'. A 'sound' is what matters most. I think in the outset it defines you as an artist. People come to recognise it as being yours, like a musical fingerprint. At that point in my career, I had no idea what my 'sound' was, or even what I wanted it to be. It was difficult to choose, because I loved so many varied genres and styles. One day I would want to sing big ballads like Celine Dion or Mariah Carey, whereas another day I would desire to have a soulful, timeless sound like Anita Baker or Randy Crawford. Then the next day I'd want to sing up-tempo R&B like Brandy or Lauren Hill. I was just so confused – who was I? And what was I destined to become? if anything!

I wasn't sure that I knew, or if I'd ever find my defining 'sound', that magical groove to creative greatness. All my influences swirled around me like a whirlpool, vying for my attention: Choose me! Choose me!

I tried to think about it some more. I'd always been inspired by strong female singers; if they have a distinctive voice then I'm like putty in their hands. The trick was to coalesce all these many influences into a coherent whole that was both original and modern. But how? All I knew was that I wanted to write great songs that were authentic and that spoke honestly to people – the Holy Grail for any artist.

I may not have known what my sound was yet, but I did know one thing: no matter how talented you are, or how good your voice is, you get nowhere without commitment and hard work. Even Mozart had to put in the hard yards (and he was a genius!) You have to be prepared to take risks, to branch out and explore. Every song is an adventure, and I was ready to start out on mine.

As Drew was a drummer as well as a producer, our collaboration quickly turned into a rock/pop ditty. It had the attitude of Kelly Clarkson laced with the Latino-style guitar featured in Christina Aguilera's *Stripped* album, which was one of my favourites at the time. Topped off by Drew's backing vocals, the track sounded like it could easily be played on American radio. It was a great effort, and by the end I was pleased I'd had the courage to spill the contents of my heart...

Excuse me for trying to be your everything
But you had me buying all of your lies and deceit
Now everything's alright and deep inside I'm over you
Although I thought it was true I was fooled, but I'm over you

After listening back to the finished track, Drew and I looked at one another, both of us clearly thinking the same thing: we were onto something good!

In a later session, we went on to write a second song together, this one called *'Control'*. It was a lot rockier than anything I'd done before; I was on a serious Girl Power kick now… Geri Halliwell would have been proud of me. Inspired by Ashlee Simpson's album *Pieces of Me*, we made sure we went all out with drum-kicks, cymbal clashes, and ball-busting guitars. I meant business, and I wanted everyone to know!

This song wasn't about the court case; this song was written to the world, to the many men who I'd already met in the music business, with all their manoeuvrings and mind games – the promises, the fakes, and the manipulators. Networking with these people was like playing a slippery game of snakes and ladders, and they always seemed to know when to throw the double six. Even though I didn't yet know what I wanted for myself, I definitely didn't appreciate middle-aged men pouring honey in my ear; telling me what to wear and how to act in order to become a successful 'Pop Princess'.

Most of the time, their vision of me as an artist was light years away from my own. At the age of seventeen, I just didn't feel comfortable being overtly sexual or slapped up in too much makeup. After having years of practise arguing with my Dad, I knew how to put up a decent fight when I wanted to. Of course, when it came to music industry types I always made sure I was very polite and sweet about my difference in opinion. While I wanted to remain true to myself, I didn't want to burn any bridges, or come over as awkward, especially not in this business.

Regardless of my sugar coating however, I could still see that it truly annoyed them when I refused to play ball. It seems that when a man stands his ground, he's labelled as assertive; he knows what he wants and he's respected for going after it. When a woman (or young woman) stands her ground, however, she's branded emotional, difficult, a bitch who thinks she knows better, a pain in the ass or even a ball-buster. Some people (men) might even say she has an attitude, and she isn't respected for it at all.

I felt strongly about this inequality, and I sang these lines with passion and sincerity – after all, they touched upon the truth:

You might just think that I'm young and naïve,

But don't be fooled by what you see

If you could see what's underneath,

You might just understand me

I know it's hard but please sympathise

'cause you don't know what it's like

Why must I always justify what I do all of the time

In my head, I was still a baby-faced singer with a love of music, just trying to figure it all out, and I hoped – in some way – that these songs would help me do that.

***

It was 6.30pm. Location: Jed's house in the hills. I was upstairs in my room, changing into an outfit I'd bought on Melrose a few days before – a black silky halter-neck top with pinstripe culottes and heels – an outfit inspired by Fergie from The Black Eyed Peas, who was my flavour of the month.

As I was putting on my shoes, the doorbell rang.

"Get that, will you?" shouted Jed from down the hall.

I rushed out and passed Dad on the landing. Suited and booted, he looked really smart; it's amazing what a shower and a suit jacket can do Dad! I ran downstairs, opened the front door, and was greeted by a small Mexican man in a chauffeur's uniform.

"Limousine booked for Vicky Nolan to go to the Staples Center for the Grammys," he said, as though the words coming out his mouth were completely normal and mundane.

The Grammys!! Wow!! Act cool, I told myself, act cool. "Yep, that's me!" I squeaked, my entire lack of cool coming across in my voice.

Dad and I walked outside towards a pearl white stretch limo that seemed to fill the whole of the drive – the car sparkled and shimmered in the afternoon sun. When the chauffeur opened the rear door we climbed in, and I slid across the seat, adjusting my outfit and making my way to the drinks cabinet – I was getting use to this by now.

Minutes later, the car pulled away from the house, beginning its journey through the canyons, along the same twisting roads that I'd power-walked that very morning. Now and then the limo's low-hanging sump caught the bottom of the uneven road with a loud metallic scrape. Ouch!

"Is ok, Is ok" came the shout from the driver at the front.

As we approached the top of the hill, Dad asked the driver,

"Could you turn onto Mulholland Drive, please? We'd like to go the scenic route; it'll make the journey extra special."

"*Si, Señor.* Whatever you want, we have time" came the polite reply.

I switched on the in-car TV, flicking through the channels until I got to MTV. It was full of manic reports about the Grammys – who's hot, who's not, who was wearing who… the usual.

I was on such a high – what teenager wouldn't be?!

We wound slowly along Mulholland, taking in the spectacular views across the valley, then easing down through Laurel Canyon, where we cruised past wrought iron entrance gates tipped with gold. Stuccoed mansions and ochre coloured Haciendas flashed by, huge estates partially hidden behind a thick curtain of greenery. These A-listers certainly knew how (and where) to live!

We reached the traffic lights at the bottom of the hill, stopping sharply at a red before hanging a left down Sunset. As if by magic the sun was doing just that, bathing the famous boulevard in a pink cocktail glow, the sky scissored with the surrounding palm trees. The occasional cerise Cadillac and lipstick-red Corvette swished by in a blur of colour.

The limo ate up the miles and soon we were on the 101-freeway pointing towards downtown LA. A cluster of huge skyscrapers loomed into view, breaking the dusk with their twinkling fairy lights – it was like driving towards one of those nocturnal picture postcards sold on Hollywood Boulevard. With my excitement growing, we entered the citadel, crawling forward intersection by intersection, into the high-tech canyons of downtown Los Angeles, its colossal towers always framing the view and peering down at us imperiously.

Leaning forwards, I asked the driver, "Where's the Staples Center, is it near?"

"Across the other side of the city, Miss. About fifteen minutes away."

Honestly, I really didn't care how long it took; I was completely lost in the fantasy of it all.

After a while we approached a large electric blue dome, which was lighting up the entire night sky in front of us. The driver turned and gestured up ahead. "The Staples Center, Miss."

Wow! It was mesmerizing; by far the glitziest arena I had ever seen. Large crowds of people were milling around and making their way inside the venue, their path criss-crossed with bright white searchlights. As we got closer I noticed that the surrounding roads were partially closed; a cluster of Highway Patrolmen in their smart beige uniforms and gold stars barred the way, vetting each car that came near them.

As our own car reached them, our driver stopped the limo, buzzing down the window and having a word with a gum-chewing marshal who directed us to an underground car park. We followed a line of polished limousines into a concrete tunnel, when suddenly a man flagged us down, telling us we could go no further. We were here.

Jumping out, we made our way towards the rear entrance of the building, an area that was choked with flashy stretch limos and shiny SUV's. These weren't, however, any ordinary stretch limos like yours truly had arrived in – oh no, they were super-duper limos stretched to infinity... massive 4X4 Cadillac Escalades and Hummers with blacked out windows and glistening spinning chrome wheels, each one containing famous artists, producers, and managers, plus entourage. It was like being in a rap music video.

The problem was, they had all arrived at the exact same time, so their drivers were vying for the best parking spots, the ones closest to the entrance. It was an intimidating battle of egos – chauffeurs beeping their horns and artists' heavies squaring up to one another, the whole ill-tempered cacophony amplified by the concrete walls and ceilings surrounding us. Talk about deadlock!

The security team – a battalion of black suited Godzilla-like bouncers with CIA like earpieces – did their best to restore order. "Hey, buddy! Stop! Wait your turn!"

One of the parked limos thrust open a rear door, causing a bevy of scantily clad dancers to spill out, followed by a Gangster Rap duo, both of whom were dripping in bling and gold chains.

Flashing our party invitations, Dad and I joined the crowd of VIP's, heading inside where the party was already in full swing. Jugglers dressed in metallic Lycra moved between the guests on stilts, dancing to the music, while urban dancers twisted and writhed around us. Fascinating displays of pop and street art adorned the walls, everything having been designed for the benefit and enjoyment of the guests, right down to the minutest napkin detail.

As we approached our seats, we wandered past row after row of buffet tables serving all types of canopies and fancy delicacies, not to mention all the champagne and cocktails. Most of the guests preferred to drink from the trendy bottled water they were clutching – maybe for some, an addition to the drugs.

The venue was split into several boxed-off areas, set aside for corporate companies and various groups of people; different genres of music, each one a party within a party. The atmosphere was buzzing, eclectic and electric. There was so much going on, I didn't know what to look at next.

One of the most interesting things I witnessed was the sight of hundreds of guys and girls wearing Stetson hats – Ten Gallon and Silverado – casually strutting around like a posse; it seemed the cowboys had come to town! And why not? Country Music is massive in the States and well represented at the Grammys, I just didn't expect quite so much of it. I also didn't expect hordes of the cowboys and girls to rush the stage the moment The Black Eyed Peas came on to entertain us; it soon became clear to me that the Grammy Awards was a real melting pot of styles, celebrating all genres of music.

The evening went by in a star-studded blur of endless people watching, awkward standing around, and meaningless chitchat with complete strangers. In the end I had neck ache from scanning the surrounding tables so much, trying to see as many celebs as I could – I didn't want to miss a thing.

Suddenly, my Blackberry pinged. I read the message, grateful to see that it wasn't from Brian, my lawyer. It was from Jed, telling me that the limo was waiting out front and that we had 'somewhere to go'. How mysterious.

Intrigued, but miffed that we were leaving, we drank up and made our way out of the arena. It was just past midnight, and I felt like Cinderella, leaving the Staples Center ball. On our way out we were handed freebie goody-bags by the PR team, of which I took two and insisted Dad did the same – free gifts all round! I thought I'd give some to my sisters.

I climbed into the limo thinking the night had come to an end, but according to Jed, it appeared it was only just beginning. On his orders, the chauffeur drove us to the Pacific Design Center in West Hollywood, known locally as the Blue Whale due to its outrageous size and skin of sparkling blue glass.

As we neared our destination – its contemporary shape jutting out above the suburban landscape getting larger and larger as we approached – once again the road became jammed with limousines, their taillights flashing like angry fireflies. Stop start! Stop start! It seemed they were all heading to the same place we were – the Warner Grammy party, held in a swanky room on the second floor, right in the belly of the Blue Whale (the same venue where Elton John holds his AIDs charity parties). All the entertainment industry's movers and shakers would be there, mingling and networking, so it made sense that we were there too.

I, however, was very unsure; it all seemed a bit unplanned, off the cuff, and I didn't feel comfortable turning up somewhere so completely unprepared. We were told we had a pass into the party, but we had no physical tickets or any contact to get us in. The instructions were: 'present yourself at reception, give your names and everything will be fine'. This didn't exactly put me at ease, I suspected we would have to blag it – I definitely had my fears, my doubts. It could be egg on face time!

"Dad, do we have to go?" I asked him, begging him, really. "We're going to look like complete fools if we get turned away!"

We sat in the traffic, both of us apprehensive, I started to shrink into the corner of the seat as each limo moved forward at a snail's pace, before finally disembarking its guests onto the red carpet. Soon – sooner than I liked – it was our turn. We moved forward, inch by inch, towards the point of no return. The car in front of us stopped, and out stepped an incredibly glamorous couple, the occasional flashlight illuminating the red carpet before them, both onlookers and paparazzi vying for the best pictures.

Suddenly, I realised we were next. I felt like a phony – after all, who was I to be walking along a red carpet with these glam people? What would they think of me?

No matter what I thought might happen, it was too late now.

The car cruised to a halt, and our driver jumped out to open the limo door. Oh God! This was it. I glanced at Dad. He glanced at me. Both of us looked like we were about to face a firing squad, Bonnie and Clyde sprang to mind. Getting out of the car, I experienced a huge – and well-needed – burst of adrenaline. Pumped full of newfound courage, we laughed nervously, egging each other on.

"Let's go for it... We can't die" Dad said, looking confident.

I nodded, taking a deep breath as I smiled back.

We stepped onto the red carpet – chin up, shoulders back, fixed grins on our faces – and strolled nonchalantly towards the lobby, camera flashes here and there blinding me in the process. Staring directly ahead, we carried on walking, not responding to the photographers trying to attract our attention – I just wanted to get into the building.

Like a slow motion bad dream, the red carpet seemed to stretch into the far distance, going on forever – would we ever make it to the end?

Finally, we got to the lobby – sanctuary! We were instantly directed up a set of stairs to the second floor, and we climbed each one with trepidation, each step seemingly taller than the last, secretly wishing we were going the other way. Upon reaching the top, we followed the other guests down a plush corridor that terminated at a reception desk manned by a small army of hospitality staff. One by one they were vetting each guest, carefully scrutinising their invitations before letting them through. We advanced towards them slowly, my adrenaline still pumping as their eyes scanned the room, eyeing up every person and mentally trying to figure them out with their stare.

We eventually got to the front of the queue, and a smartly dressed lady with a big beaming smile presented herself to us. "Good evening. Your names, please?"

"Vicky Nolan and Kevin Nolan," Dad announced confidently, nodding his head as he spoke.

The lady scanned the list, up and down, page by page. Upon reaching the end – with no sign of our names – she looked at us suspiciously before turning back to page one and starting all over again.

I was starting to feel very uncomfortable now, not to mention a bit sweaty… how humiliating. I glanced over my shoulder, trying to appear natural and not at all embarrassed. Oh God… a long line of guests had now backed up behind us, some of them tutting impatiently. There were probably some serious music execs in that queue, desperate to get in and start drinking the tequila, and here we were, trying to crash a party and holding them all up in the process!

The lady checking the list glanced at her colleague, then turned to us and said, politely but firmly, "No. Your names aren't on here. Who invited you?"

"Jed Chankin," Dad mumbled. I nodded in agreement. "Would you please excuse me for a moment? I need to make a call."

Dad and I shuffled away sheepishly, although secretly, I was relieved. There would be no more fake small talk, no more trying to approach people who didn't have a clue who I was. I felt the tenseness in my shoulders and neck ease; I didn't have to pretend to be somebody else anymore – I could just be me and go to bed dreaming of the glitzy night we'd enjoyed. One day maybe, my name would be on the list to that hot industry party, but not tonight.

We moved towards the exit, calmly at first, then gradually quickening our pace. As we hurried back down the red carpet, our complexions matched it perfectly – I felt like my face was flushed bright red.

Still, I tried to focus on the positives: I knew we could head back to the comfort of the house and pretend this whole embarrassing thing had never happened.

I just hoped Jed would understand.

Tongue tied, occupied in my mind again
Running fast, coming last since I don't know when
I, I don't know why…
False start, tripping over myself again
Hit the ground, look around, want to fly again
Up, up, up away in the sky
Take me over land and sea
Take me over and find me
Wings lift me up above
To soar and glide, I'm taking off

Glimpses of me… Coffee Shop

Time to wake up and smell the coffee!

Now, I like the smell of coffee, but not the taste. My best ever, most favourite hot drink is actually hot chocolate – double choc and whipped cream plus lots of lovely marshmallows. Now that's a drink.

I jump on the tube and head for my favourite coffee shop in Soho. After walking along Wardour Street – the epicentre of the British film industry – I turn left and I'm there.

It's one of those old-fashioned coffee shops with a zinc counter, onyx tables, and raffia chairs, the walls crammed with black and white photos of Soho in the sixties. Legend has it that Mick Jagger used to pop in for a double espresso on his way to rehearsals. No wonder he can't stop moving!

You open the door and the first thing that hits you is the rich aroma of ground coffee beans. Well, that and the splash-and-steam of the ancient dispenser. Then it's the Romeo baristas in their white shirts and black aprons, with their wise guy chit-chat and flirty come-ons.

The place is full but luckily, I find a seat by the window. I sit down, put my mug on a paper doily, and scan the room. The clientele is a disparate bunch – creative types, PR people, tourists, and market traders. Murmured conversation percolates the air.

After catching my breath, I open my bag. By now I've got the routine of waiting for a meeting down to a fine art: I take a sip of hot chocolate, reach for my iPhone, plug in my earbuds, and select my favourite music on Spotify. At the moment, it's Lissie's album Catching a Tiger. Very Fleetwood Mac-esque.

9

Brooklyn… is that the bridge?

Brash, colourful shops, fast food outlets, hotels and nightclubs, casinos, and bars. It's a little rough around the edges and at night it blazes brightly with thousands of glowing electrified glass tubes.

Sound familiar? No, it's not Las Vegas, but 'Basvegas', as the locals affectionately call it – a large retail park a few miles outside Basildon, Essex, England.

We'd driven all the way down from Manchester for a recording session with two up-and-coming songwriters and producers that I had met on Myspace – Zach Charlton and Darren Green, my new musical collaborators – 200 miles travel non-stop by car (torture!) – we made our way to the hotel, my legs still tired and contorted as we checked in late into the Travelodge.

My room overlooked a sprawling car park but I was too tired to notice; I crashed onto the bed for an hour before heading off to the studio. I had no idea what to expect.

It was just an ordinary house on an ordinary street on the outskirts of Basildon, and Zach (from Liverpool) and Darren (an Islington boy) were standing outside when we got there. Cue big hugs and handshakes.

They opened the garage door and we all walked in, squeezing past an old lawn mower and making our way to a room at the back of the house. Their home studio was understated – small and neat, with do-it-yourself soundproofing, a mini mixing desk, mic stands, and a few instruments scattered about on bean cushions. Good things come in small packages, right?

After a quick shot of caffeine to buzz the brain, we got down to the fun part of writing and recording. The boys were a dream to work with, Zach's wicked Scouse humour complimenting Darren's 'Landon' manner. They were open for business and very friendly, and over a two-day period, we managed to pen *Here Now, Look Out of Your Window, and Mr So Sure* – it just goes to show you don't need to book into a fancy recording studio to make good music and hit it off with someone.

The last night we all went for a meal, first taking a walk around downtown Basvegas. Like its big brother out in the Nevada desert, Basvegas has a real Jekyll and Hyde quality; as the daylight fades it sparks in to a haze of light, and *voila!* The retail park is transformed into Basildon's version of the Vegas Strip. The high rollers (and the low!) are drawn in from the surrounding towns and villages like big spender party animals – it saves getting the train into expensive London, so why not!

Nando's was our chosen eatery, and we slid in to sit at a table by the window, overlooking the floodlit car park.

"Four Piri Piri Chicken, please all with rice and corn-on-the-cobs. Thanks."

We chatted about music and how the recording sessions went, and the sweet harmonies we had created, and when the food came – it fell on me that we'd all ordered chicken, and that we were all in eating in harmony – I was reminded of a funny scene from *The Simpsons TV Show*. It went a bit like this; Homer was preaching to a group of Hindus, Muslims, Jews, and Christians, talking about how we should all come together. He says, 'Look, we're not going to eat cow, and we're not going to eat pork, but hey, everybody likes chicken!' And they all agree.

It seems Homer was right: we all want harmony, and we all want chicken.

***

A pale, ghostly light filtered through the hotel blinds as vague shapes coalesced in front of me; a desk, an armchair, a flat screen TV. As tired as I was, I couldn't wait to wake up in the city that never sleeps.

I stumbled out of bed, bleary-eyed, transatlantic jetlag clawing at my brain, and pulling the window-cord, I sliced open the blind – *swish!* – allowing the winter sunlight to stream in.

The view from the top floor was fixating. I'd seen it a million times on TV but I'd never actually seen it for real… Awesome! Across the Hudson River, the iconic Manhattan skyline stretched out before me, a Lego landscape of densely-packed skyscrapers, all of them partially shrouded in mist.

It was February and I was staying at the Sheraton Meadowlands in New Jersey – one of those large, modern, purpose-built hotels favoured by out-of-town businessmen and tourists on a budget. The area was semi-industrial, a featureless landscape, ringed by spaghetti-like freeway intersections and still drab waterways. Down below, a group of men huddled around a smoking brazier in a workyard. Trucks came and went at all hours of the day.

We were there to meet Jay Rosen, a New York attorney who'd 'friended' me on MySpace and who had told me he was a 'fan', having discovered me first on YouTube – it's true, the world is getting smaller and smaller. Basically, Jay messaged me and said it would be "a pleasure and an honour to represent you Stateside". Kind words indeed. "Hey!" he'd added. "Why not fly to New York? I'll arrange some meetings and introduce you to some people."

It seemed like an opportunity that was too good to miss, plus I've always wanted to see New York City, so I agreed to go and he told me to phone him the moment I hit town. So, I did, and this was why I was leaving him a message on his answering machine.

"Hi Jay! I'm here, finally, as promised. I'm looking forward to seeing you, please call me when you pick up this message, bye!"

Now I was waiting for him to call back, waiting and hoping that he *would* call back. Surely, he would, right?

I stepped back from the window, sat down on the bed, and

stared at my phone, willing it to ring.

It wasn't ringing.

Why won't it ring? I kept asking myself, glancing at my watch every now and then to see how much time had gone by. Twenty minutes passed, then another twenty, then another, but still there was no call.

As time went on, I got more and more pensive, and then the doubts started to creep into my mind. *What if he doesn't ring at all? What if he just blanks me? Maybe he's a time waster? Maybe he isn't for real? Maybe I've flown all the way here to New York for diddly-squat! What a sucker!!*

Just then, Dad came in. "Has he rung, Vic?"

"No."

"He will."

"What if he doesn't?"

"He will, Vic."

"But what if he…" I trailed off when I heard my phone ring, and looking down at the display, I saw it was Jay, Relief!

After talking to him for a few minutes, we jumped into the hire car and headed off down the New Jersey turnpike. It was bitterly cold and very windy, the sky a bright ice blue.

"Where are we meeting him?" Dad asked me as we went.

"Soho, downtown, in an Italian restaurant called Mardi's. It's not until later though, so we've got plenty of time for sightseeing."

Dad smiled, tapping the address of the restaurant into the GPS. My Dad decided to stay in New Jersey because he wanted to sample real 'New York' life. He was just as relieved as I was that the meeting was taking place. More so considering the money he'd spent getting us there. To come all that way for nothing would have been a difficult pill to swallow.

Gas stations, derelict warehouses, and five-and-dime stores flashed by – it was like driving through a chorus of a Springsteen song. We took the exit for the Lincoln Tunnel, following a line of cars descending under the Hudson River. It was slow and congested, the weariness of the morning commute etched onto people's faces.

Picking up speed, we hit the ramp and exited the tunnel. Bright daylight announced we were now in midtown Manhattan, and while its chasm of skyscrapers barricaded the sun, along the arrow-straight avenues it broke through here and there in golden bands of light thrown across busy intersections, crisscrossed in shadow.

I gazed up at the sheer cliff face of concrete and glass, an awesome manmade canyon crowded with taxis, cars, and commuters. High on the thrill of it, we opened the sunroof and charged down the avenues, dashing from stop light to stop light, taking in the sights as we moved along.

We were laughing and singing, honking our horn in unison with the friendly yellow cabs as Dad jumped from lane to lane. It felt great being there, with the car's CD player blaring out... Prefab Sprout... *Hey Manhattan!* How do you do?

Slowly, the late afternoon sun began to set, its slanting rays bathing the city in a delicate gold. Soon the avenues and sidewalks were plunged into shadow, while above, the tallest skyscrapers flared like crystal torches, dazzling in the sun's final embrace.

We skirted Central Park and drove south towards Soho, a bohemian district so hip and cool it hurt. Lights were coming on all over the city as we parked opposite a bagel bakery and made our way along the sidewalk to Mardi's Italian restaurant. As taxis swished by, puffs of steam emanated from metal grids like ghosts.

Passing under a curved archway, we were greeted by a waiter who showed us to the bar, and it wasn't long before Jay appeared. I could tell straight away it was him: young, good-looking, and sharp suited, he oozed New York swagger and attitude – that strange mixture of street-savvy charm and slick boardroom bolero.

After scanning the place for a second, he marched straight over towards me, a warm, killer smile on his face as he greeted us in his soft Noo Yawk accent, "Hi, Vicky. Jay Rosen. I recognise you from your Myspace page," he said laughing before adding, "Great to meet you," as he pecked me on both cheeks. "This must be your Dad?"

"Hi Mate," said Dad, in a conspicuous Manchester twang.

Jay shook his hand, motioned towards me, and grinned. "You gotta love this gal. She flies all the way to New York faster than a bullet – I'm so pleased you came."

After signalling to the waiter, Jay led us into a quaint cobbled courtyard, decked out with dining tables covered with red check tablecloths, each with its own candle burning atop an empty bottle of wax-streaked *Chianti*. It was like walking onto the set of an old gangster movie.

We sat beneath a spreading canopy of vines and blossoms festooned with twinkling fairy lights, as old Roman busts stared down at us from corner plinths. Accordion music was piped *alfresco*. If it wasn't for the chill night air, you'd swear you were on holiday in the Med.

During the meal, I found out four main things Jay was keen to tell me about – 1: he was Jewish. 2: he'd once worked for legendary music magnate, Russell Simmons, co-founder of the hip-hop label, Def Jam Records. 3: he was a massive Jamiroquai fan. And 4: he had a peculiar interest in Benjamin Franklin, which he told me quite a lot about. I never knew Benjamin Franklin was a storm chaser; apparently, he used to chase after tornadoes on horseback. You learn something new every day!

Jay told us all about life at Def Jam: the ins and outs at the label, the latest business trends, the current roster of rap artist, he really knew his stuff. Since then, after feeling that the time was right, he'd branched out on his own.

He explained that he wanted his own stable of artists – which was why he'd contacted me – and he started giving me the lowdown, his words silvery smooth. "I run a small boutique agency downtown. Very select. I only deal with the *crème de la crème*."

He took a sip of his espresso. "I'd love to work with you Vicky, so I'd like you to meet a good friend of mine who I think could be good for us, I've made a reservation to meet him tomorrow lunchtime at TAO, just off 6th Ave, Asian food? Sounds good?"

"Yeah thanks, sounds good, hey, we have a meeting at Reprise over on 6th tomorrow morning, we'll meet afterwards"

"Sounds like a plan" Jay replied.

That night, snuggling down in my Sheraton duvet, I dozed off to the sound of police sirens wailing in downtown Hoboken. Just before I fell asleep, however, a very important thought occurred to me: I hadn't gone shopping yet! Telling myself I'd put that right the next day, I drifted into a restful sleep.

The morning after, a gorge of cold wind and driving showers whipped through the skyscrapers, buffeting a group of New Yorkers who were shivering at an intersection. The lights changed and they charged across en-masse, struggling with their umbrellas – Dad and I were watching from the heated comfort of our car.

We were back in Manhattan, making our way to the meeting at Rockefeller Plaza. Parking was a problem there, a real 'Pain in the a**' as the locals – who all took the subway instead – would say. It was so overcrowded you either had to park your car up or down: down in an underground parking lot, or up in a parking elevator. Up is tricky, but a lot more entertaining!

I had no idea such places existed until we discovered one wedged between two office blocks. What happens is, you drive in, park in a steel cage, and get out. Your car is then picked up automatically and elevated skywards to its place – a kind of Thunderbirds lift contraption, or a Rubik's Cube for cars. It's mind-bending, I couldn't help but stare, seeing all these cars shelved one on top of another in rows of six to ten deep. It really is a space-age use of space, and I'd never seen one of those in the UK before. What America does today...

We made our way to the offices of Reprise Records and as I'd put on my pop star look, I was ready and psyched up for the meeting. I mean, we were talking about the very same record label set up by Frank Sinatra! 'Start spreadin' the news…' bring it on! Raymond McGlamery and A&R exec Tommy Page were waiting for us in reception, and after a quick meet and greet and a whirl around the label departments we made the short walk uptown for lunch at TAO, for our next appointment with Jay and his business associate Bill Dinah.

Formerly a balconied movie theatre, the massive space had been transformed into an Asian temple, seating hundreds of diners.

The first thing you see when you walk in is a huge towering Buddha that floats majestically above a glass fish tank – the pond faintly babbling below. Red and white Koi carp slowly swim around in the water, occasionally coming to the surface to feed, and the whole place is decorated with green vegetation and silver leafed bamboo trees, the walls and ceilings stripped back and festooned with oriental artefacts. Moreover, the smells of pungent spices waft in the air, adding to the whole sense of the mystical east – this sure wasn't the Chinese take-away on Park Lane in Poynton.

We met Jay and Bill and were efficiently ushered to our booth in the VIP area by our hostess (who was dressed in a black kimono), the menus arrived, and the food quickly followed. Between mouthfuls of mouth-watering Bang Bang chicken salad and soy-glazed salmon we chatted about the music business and New York, and yes, I felt like I knew it all, sitting there and mixing with the razzle-dazzle of the New York diners.

Of course, that didn't last much longer, as right then I made a terrible *faux pas*, which sent me crashing very quickly down to earth.

"So, Vicky," said Bill Dinah, Jay's friend, the music exec, "Now you're here in New York, what's the one thing you really wanna do?"

"Well," I answered, confidently, "Well Bill, I'm looking forward to seeing the Big Apple."

He tilted his head, looking puzzled. "What do you mean?"

"I want to see the Big Apple, Bill," I said, unsure how much clearer I could be, "where is it?"

"Vicky," he replied, smiling at my naivety, "you're *in* the Big Apple right now!"

Jay and Dad looked at one another, they smirked, then broke into a fit of giggles.

Well, maybe I didn't know everything after all!

***

Macy's! Let me tell you about Macy's – it's far less embarrassing.

After lunch, Dad and I popped into the world-famous store on West 34th Street for a bit of retail therapy, and believe me, I needed it after the TAO slip up!

Luckily for me, there were SALE signs everywhere, something that very much set my pulse racing. Unlike UK SALES, however – where the shoppers are offered bin-end dregs – in America it's high-end designer stuff that tends to make it to the till register.

So, I dived in enthusiastically, losing myself amidst the clothes racks and make-up aisles and jewellery counters, with Bobbi Brown and MAC… and, well, you get the picture. Poor Dad didn't stand a chance; he trailed forlornly behind me like a lost sheep, powerless to stop my shopping binge. Ah…. heaven!

"Yes, I'm done thank you, please ring me up" – as the Americans would say at the till register.

10

A mad tea party

The female security guard looked me straight in the eye as she announced, "Please empty your personal belongings into the tray."

I did as I was told and quick as a flash, my phone, keys, handbag and purse whizzed down a carousel into the belly of the scanner, emerging on the other side just moments later.

The guard beckoned me forward to walk through the metal detector, a buzz sounding the moment I hit the invisible beam.

"It's probably the belt," I said, as she ushered me through, an unreadable expression on her face.

I raised my arms as instructed, standing there surrendering as she wafted the handheld detector around the contours of my body. Luckily, it didn't make a sound.

"OK, you can go through now," she replied, her face sour and still showing no sign of emotion.

I was back inside the hallowed portals of Manchester High Court for day two of my trial, and straight away I was met by the same familiar odour – that nauseating smell of musty corridors, polished wood, and the ever-present fearful sense of authority.

I waited as Mum and Dad finished passing through security, both of them looking staid and tired and after a night of little sleep. The lead-up to the trial was taking its toll and while Mum worked in corporate hospitality, in a job that required a bubbly personality and a sunny disposition, I still didn't know how she was managing to smile her way through all of this. Greeting customers and clients like she didn't have a care in the world and seeing to their every need, while in the background, day by day, a nagging sense of uncertainty was slowly eating away at her and her family. I thought she deserved an Oscar for her performance.

And then there was Dad, trying to run his small interior decorating business whilst juggling a blizzard of letters and phone calls from lawyers and barristers. The complex legal issues, the intricate jargon, but most of all, the thinly-veiled threats. It was hard to see him going through it – after all, he was just an ordinary bloke. Like a million other dads out there, he simply wanted the best for his daughter and family. Now he was faced with a trial that was threatening to destroy the family-life we had, our lives hanging by a thread. If we were to lose, we would most certainly lose the house, maybe even a change of school, it was awful, but there wasn't anything we could do to change it. That's just what it's like when you enter the labyrinth of the law; you surrender all control and plunge headlong into the quicksand.

I just hoped the judge would see common sense and strike out all this nonsense. Please!

After security, we went into the public cafeteria for an informal meeting with our lawyer and barrister. What was peculiar was seeing the barristers resplendent in their wigs and gowns, deep in quiet conversation with people dressed in their smartest clothes, all of it taking place around shabby ubiquitous tables, like the type you'd find in tired old government buildings and schools.

It was obvious from their body language that deep serious discussions were taking place, it seemed rather incongruous that these meetings weren't being held in private, rather than in this very public space, the cafeteria, with its tea ladies, clattering teacups and scraping chairs. I scanned the room trying to lip-read their conversations and interrogations, though without much success. The whole thing had a nightmarishly, Kafkaesque quality about it.

I caught the eye of our barrister, Amanda Michaels, and our lawyer, Brian Drewitt, both of whom waved us over. I'd chosen a female barrister because I felt we would make a connection after she complimented me on my handbag – girl power and all that. Though in all honesty, most the other male lawyers and barristers we'd come across had come up short, so on a notion I thought a female barrister might pull through for me. It was certainly worth a shot.

The previous time we had met I'd had the chance to chat with her and I appreciated her empathy and professionalism; she was polished and self-assured, and seemed to have a handle on all aspects of my case. She was also a straight talker with a no-nonsense attitude – something that seemed lacking from the others before her. I liked her a lot. I felt much more confident having such a strong woman in my corner, though of course, only time would tell.

We sat at the table, each of us taking a cup of tea, and then we got down to business. Straight away Amanda was on the case: "I've been told by their counsel that they're prepared to negotiate and settle. I understand a quarter of a million pounds plus costs has been mentioned. If you pay this sum, then the case is over and we can all walk away."

A QUARTER OF A MILLION POUNDS?

I nearly choked on my tea, trying hard not to let it spurt out of my nose and land on Amanda's Filofax. "I'm still in sixth form college and work part time at Tesco… TESCO!" I replied, almost shouting. "I'm still doing my exams! Is he on another planet?! All of this manoeuvring and time wasting meant my life was on hold, in limbo because of these people… This is madness!! How is this fair?" I was deflated, almost crying.

Everyone was staring at me blankly. It seemed there were no words left – we'd exhausted them all.

Finally, we started discussing the issues at hand; we all knew it was too late for negotiation and that payment to them was not a realistic proposition, so we put that down. I kept sipping my tea.

After the discussion, Brian and Amanda got to their feet, Brian gathering up his heavy files, court documents, and papers in readiness for the morning's proceedings.

As he left the table holding his suitcase and heavy files, he remarked eloquently in his old school, courteous manner, "Let them trouser your hard-earned money? Not on Drewitt's watch, they won't!"

I already liked Brian, but now I liked him even more.

Suddenly, the in-house PA system interrupted the hubbub of the cafeteria as a woman in clipped English tones announced, "All interested parties to Court 2a please... All interested parties to Court 2a... Arkace Leobright versus Nolan... Arkace Leobright versus Nolan..."

Here we go again, I thought.

Our family stood up as one, our chairs screeching loudly on the cafeteria floor, like nails scraping a chalkboard, the din drawing unwanted attention from the surrounding tables. This was our cue to get a move on: it was time to face my ex-manager again.

I wasn't looking forward to it – not at all – but another day in the witness box meant we were getting closer to this being over.

I just hoped we'd win.

***

We were standing on the platform of Heron's Quay station waiting for the Docklands Light Railway to whisk us into town – London Town – and we weren't alone; the place was thronged with city commuters, reading newspapers and chatting noisily on their mobiles.

I craned my neck, squinting up at the famous Canary Wharf skyscrapers – the Barclays and HSBC towers – dazzling in the morning sun. It was hot and clammy, the light hurting my eyes, and as I looked down, the bright red dockland train rolled in and rattled into the station, followed by a welcoming draught of cooler air.

We all squeezed aboard through the narrow doors, a rather civilised surge that epitomised the regular London city commute.

I was there with Dad and singer/songwriter Richie Dews. Richie really embodied what it meant to be a musician: he carried a show-stopping guitar case, wore rock star leather and he had *amazing* hair. He didn't have the nickname '*Rock Star*' for nothing, and he certainly stood out amidst all those suits!

The train pulled away from the station, snaking its way into London. We were heading for Leicester Square, to the Café de Paris – the famed music venue, where Richie and I would be performing a short set later that evening. Richie was my guitarist extraordinaire and someone I had written songs with over the past couple of years.

I'd been told that the crowd at the Café de Paris had a reputation for being loud and raucous, but that didn't worry Richie; he fronted his own rock band and was used to being on stage in front of loons and boisterous crowds, the women throwing their underwear at him and the men throwing their beer! He was my wingman today, something that made me feel confident and secure; we always had a good laugh and he always had my back when we performed. I couldn't ask for anyone better.

After a few stops we disembarked at Bank Station, being pushed and jostled by a hectic crowd of city workers and tourists, we moved at speed through the underground station, up and down steep escalators as we headed towards the Piccadilly Line.

Boy oh boy it was oppressive and clammy in there; draughts of warm air whooshed up the escalator shafts and the interconnecting tiled-tunnels, a sickly mix of body odour, heady perfume, and engine lubricants. The mournful cry of a busker echoed along the tunnels. Piped music! Only a few people stopped to give him change, not including us – we were in a rush and had to scurry past as I threw him a quick glance.

Finally, we jumped off at Leicester Square, Ritchie's guitar case catching the coat of a fellow commuter. Of course, the usual English pleasantries were exchanged:

"Sorry."

"No, no, it was my fault."

"Sorry again."

"…Sorry."

Zooming up the escalator, we were carried by the human tide into the main body of the station, and one by one we fed our Oyster Cards into the barrier system. Moments later, we pushed through and made our way out into the crowded daylight of Leicester Square. Freedom! Fresh air! Sunlight! Pigeons dive-bombed and scattered, and I was all hot and bothered. I was glad I didn't have to do *that* every day!

Straight away, we headed for the Café de Paris on nearby Coventry Street, from the outside the famous old nightclub looked a tad inconspicuous; a tiny entrance painted black with gold rococo lettering above the door.

But as I knew, you shouldn't judge a book by its cover, and once I entered the building and headed down a set of carpeted stairs, the full majesty of the place became apparent: it was like stepping back in time to *Le Belle Époque* Paris, its opulent decor and burlesque glamour giving it a slightly seedy, dangerous feel.

First opened in 1924, the venue had played host to countless megastars such as Frank Sinatra, Grace Kelly, and Nöel Coward, not to mention half of London's gangsters. Looking around at its interior, it wasn't hard to imagine.

Moments later we were met by Patrick Mclean, the senior A&R guy from indie record label, Upper 11 Records. It was Patrick who'd made tonight's showcase gig possible, and he also wanted to sign me, but I hadn't yet made my mind up – they were an unknown quantity and I wanted to check them out first.

He met me at the bar before taking us on a quick tour of the place, something I very much enjoyed; it was an amazing venue, with circular dance floor fronting a stage that was emblazoned with a Café de Paris lantern sign and flanked by two gold staircases. The eye was drawn upwards to an ornate carved metal balcony, and then further still to a huge crystal chandelier that glittered against the blue and claret satin ceiling like a whole galaxy of stars.

After the tour, Patrick led us to a suite of private rooms set aside for tonight's performers. Talk about atmospheric – they were dimly lit and decorated with silken drapes and red velvet upholstery, an inferno of crimsons and clarets everywhere you looked. Candelabras, chandeliers, and gold baroque mirrors added to the faded grandeur, and the room had a fragrant woody smell about it. Looking around me, I felt like I was in the movie *Moulin Rouge*.

Sound check time! Richie and I took to the stage, and just before we launched into our first song, Patrick joined us for a chat. Apparently, we'd been shunted to first place in the running order.

Ritchie was having none of it. "No way we're going on first! I know we're from the North, but sliced breads arrived there too! We want the middle order at least or we're off for a drink," he shouted, meaning: Adios! We'll be drinking with the tourists outside in Leicester Square.

Patrick sighed, giving us an awkward smile. "OK, guys. Leave it with me. I'll see what I can do."

So, we left it with him, and while I wasn't holding out much hope, we later found out that we'd been pushed-up to third on the bill. Richie always knew what was best and when people were taking the micky!

The evening soon rolled around, and after getting changed, I wandered into the venue to check out the crowd. Most were congregated at the bar, but some had already taken their seats and tables. The atmosphere was building nicely.

Half an hour later, the MC announced my name, and Richie and I jumped onstage, grabbing our mics in a squeal of feedback. My heart raced as Ritchie plugged in his guitar – a cool retro green one that suited his edgy demeanour – and started stabbing out a few chords.

The spotlight swung across the stage, hitting me perfectly. "Hello everyone!" I announced. "My name's Vicky Nolan and this is my guitarist Richie Dews, thank you for having me here tonight. We hope you enjoy the songs."

Luckily, the audience clapped and whooped – always a good

sign. With that, we launched into our short set, and I knocked out the songs with everything I had. We started with an upbeat track we wrote called *Hit the Sunshine* to get the crowd warmed up, following it with a couple more up-tempo tunes and finishing with the mellowest of vibes, a song called *All So Beautiful* – a twinkly little ditty that really showcased my voice.

It was a short set that went down well with the crowd, and both Richie and I were made up – after all, both of us knew how hard London audiences were to please. For the first time in a long while I was comfortable, and yes, not nervous!

An appreciative round of applause broke out as we left the stage, and we were free to go off and enjoy the rest of the evening, London style, along with my friends Zach and Darren who'd come down from Essex to support me.

I'd learnt a valuable lesson that night, when you're gigging and you're pushed down the performance line-up, don't settle for the crust, instead insist on a sliced loaf! ... and don't forget to bring your own wingman, Hey Maverick... Hey Richie!!

Glimpses of Me... If Food Be the Music of Love, Eat On

It's 6.30 p.m. and I'm sitting alone in my boyfriend's flat in Dalston, London. Time to think about all things culinary – I last ate at lunchtime but now I'm STARVING. I may be a slim but I have a big appetite! I'm waiting to see my lovely boyfriend, Ed; the beau of my life. I last saw him rushing out of the door this morning on his way to an important meeting at work. We first met on MySpace where he found my music and me. Sparks didn't fly immediately, but at some point, something clicked and… that was it!

There's the sound of a key in the latch and then the door swings open. Ed walks in wearing a big smile and his favourite flat-cap.

We embrace. "How was your day?"

"Great! How was yours?"

There's that magical feeling of reconnecting after a long day, the split-second pause as our eyes meet.

"I'm starving!" says Ed.

We go into the kitchen and do our usual thing – prepare and share a meal. A dash of ketchup – a dash of love – perfect!

You look good in love

Oh it was made for you

It fits you like a well cut suit

There's no denying, cause I feel it too

Let's go go go, you got me plead

Baby I'm begging you, youre what I'm needing

Oh oh oh my heart's on my sleeve…

11

It's all in the producer's mix…

The Nolan family home is a pretty Victorian house set in the beautiful Cheshire countryside. Built of red brick, it features Georgian sash windows and has lovely views looking across the surrounding greenbelt, its rolling fields inhabited with sheep and horses plus the occasional scavenging fox. The house has a lovely old-fashioned porch fretted in black and white timber, with a pair of coach lamps flanking the sturdy olive green front door.

From the moment you enter, you find yourself wrapped in northern hospitality: *"Would you like a cup of tea, love? Can I get you a croissant or a French Fancy? We have loads of them! Dad's just cleared the entire reduced aisle at Asda…"* These kinds of questions are the norm for my house, and I like it that way.

I realise how lucky I was to grow up in such a lovely home, being brought up by loving parents who worked very hard to give me and my sisters a good, solid start in life. My parents' own childhoods were a far cry from the cosy, middle class idyll enjoyed by my sisters and I, especially my Dad having come from virtually nothing – his life shaped by his poor Mancunian upbringing, they were all too aware of how easily things can be lost – all too aware of the wolf scratching at the door, ready to sink its teeth into the heart of the family without a second thought, instantly destroying everything they'd worked so hard for.

It was a crisp autumn morning when the wolf first made its appearance – 7 a.m. to be precise, the exact time that a trio of sinister-looking men dressed in black overcoats were crunching up the drive with determined stealth.

I was upstairs in bed, blissfully unaware of what was about to happen, when *BANG! BANG! BANG!* went the Victorian brass door knocker, making me bolt upright. Who the hell was at the door at this time in the morning? Our German Shepherd Heidi had obviously thought the same thing, as she started barking out an alarm call that echoed throughout the whole house.

Instead of leaving it to Mum and Dad, I rushed down the stairs in my pyjamas – with some pretty serious bed-head hair going on – closely followed by a rather confused-looking Mum, cradling baby Elizabeth in her arms.

As I opened the front door I tried to adjust my dressing gown to cover my childish pyjamas, and through the glaze of my sleepy eyes, I focused in on the men in front of me. They were stern-faced bouncer types; the kind you'd see on rough nightclub doors.

One carried a clipboard and they all wore the officious expression of the heartless loan shark. My heart paced faster.

"Y, yes?" I stammered, wondering who they were and what the hell they wanted with us at silly o'clock.

One of the men – who resembled a bald Hulk Hogan – thrust his ID badge into my face. "Are you Vicky Nolan?" he asked, no smile, no nothing.

"Yes?"

"My name is Mr Knave," he informed me, with no hint of warmth in his voice at all. "I'm an enforcement officer sent from the High Court. These men are my colleagues. I'm here to inform you that we've been sent by the High Court to execute a writ..." He looked down at his clipboard. "Arkace Ltd and Leobright Ltd claimants... defendants, Vicky Nolan and Kevin Nolan... Judgment Debt and costs to pay, £1,813 and 22 pence."

My brain was struggling to process what I was hearing. "Sorry?" I asked, staring at his clipboard in confusion.

"Can you pay this debt?" was all he said.

Eh? Debt? Just then, the seriousness of the situation hit me. A barrage of confusing thoughts whirled around my brain, just like in the movies when someone has a flashback of images speeding through their mind. The shock sharpened my senses, making everything faster and hyper-real; I heard the dog barking non-stop, I could trace the branching capillaries in the man's bloodshot eyes, and I could smell the stale cigarette smoke on his tailored overcoat. My mind was in overdrive, completely overloaded with information.

"Not right now, I can't," I said eventually. "Of course, I can't pay! I don't understand. Why are my manager's companies wanting money now? We're still at Court. Nobody's won yet, it isn't over!"

"Well, that may be true, Miss Nolan," replied Mr Knave, "but today I'm instructed by the High Court to collect, and if you can't pay, we'll have to take goods to the value of £1,813 and 22 pence." He looked towards the drive, pointing to Dad's car, before turning back and pointing in my face. "I have the power to take the car if necessary."

He wasn't bluffing. These guys weren't going anywhere.

I peered over his shoulder and saw a low-loader car transporter parked on the road, next to a line of vehicles that the men had apparently arrived in. The driver was leaning out of the cab window, just waiting for the signal to take Dad's car. He looked rough and uncompromising, it meant nothing to him.

Mum – who had been silent until now – let out a sigh of anguish, Elizabeth then woke up and immediately started crying. – expecting an early feed, no doubt.

It was hard to take in what was happening. One minute I'd been lying in bed half asleep, and the next minute three men who'd consumed a few too many protein shakes were standing on my doorstep, demanding money and threatening my family. I felt small and powerless. It all seemed a bit over-the-top. Take her down and throw away the key! Off with their heads! *No, your honour, noooooo!*

Upon hearing the commotion, Dad came quickly into the hall. "What's going on? Who are you?" he asked, a perplexed expression across his face.

The enforcement officer explained the situation for a second time, turning his sights on Dad. "I'm sorry, but if I don't get payment I'll have to take the car."

"This is a ******* joke! Wait there a minute; just wait there, I'm calling my lawyer."

Dad left us on the doorstep, hotfooting it into the lounge to ring our lawyer, Brian.

When he told him what was going on, Brian was livid. "This is totally out of order, Kevin. Costs are settled *after* the court case is heard, not *during!* They're trying to put pressure you."

"What should I do? They've threatened to take the car."

Brian thought for a moment, his legal brain swiftly computing the whys-and-wherefores of the situation. "I realise it's not fair Kevin, but for the time being I think it's best if you pay them. I'll ring the court office later to see what's gone on and try to sort things out."

Still incredibly annoyed, Dad came back into the hall with his credit card, reluctantly paying them every penny and putting the family into even more debt.

We watched angrily as the men got into their cars and drove away, followed moments later by the empty low-loader.

Later on, that day, Brian phoned Dad to explain that a lawyer's protocol hadn't been properly observed between the parties, and ungentlemanly conduct was mentioned (in other words, the gloves were off and they were trying to intimidate us).

Typical! These guys were all making it up as they went along; meaning, the whole unpleasant experience had simply been a 'misunderstanding'. How comforting…

I remember at times during the case we kind of joked about it, but deep down it hurt me, it made me realise how real it all was, and I feared for next time the bailiffs might call, looking for more than money.

All I could think was: please, please, let it end and go away.

I just hoped it would all be over soon; they may have taken away our money that day, but there was one thing they could never take away from us: hope.

Let me hear you say, put them up, put them up.

Let me hear you say, put them up, put them up.

For every finger you point, there's are three pointing back at you.

For every chance that you let slip by, you've got a lame excuse

It's time for bravery, we'll fight the good fight… the good fight.

INT. VICTORIAN TERRACE HOUSE. HAMPSTEAD. DAYTIME.

VICKY standing around in the bathroom in front of an impromptu mic stand. It is quiet, the only noise; tap dripping in the sink

DECONZO a cool hip US record producer in his twenties, sits opposite his laptop/improvised music studio in a bedroom. He's

tapping at his keyboard - setting up the recording session.

                    DECONZO
   Vicky! Can you hear me in there? In your
                    super-

   duper cool sound booth... err bathroom!!
                  (laughter!)

                    VICKY
     Yep, loud and clear... in the loo!
                  (laughter!)

                    DECONZO
     So that's what you Brits call the
              bathroom, the loo!
   (more laughter) Cans OK? Can you hear the
                    track?

                      139

                    VICKY
              Yep, all good...

                   DECONZO
       Give me something, voice or something...

                    VICKY
        Testing... one two... one two... la...
                      la...

VICKY looks around and notices the tap
dripping faster in the bathroom sink.
DECONZO puts his music headphones on.

                   DECONZO
       Right Vicky, nearly ready to put something
                     down.

DECONZO pushes some of the sliders on a
small music console.

                   DECONZO
         Ready Vic, here goes... gimme sweet
                    music...

                    VICKY
             Will do, Go for it...

VICKY gets into the groove, head nodding in
time to the beat

                    VICKY

(singing) want to let you know... how much
                  I care

                   DECONZO

  Whoa!... Whoa! wait a minute Vic,
            something wrong

                    VICKY

               What's up?

                   DECONZO

I can hear something, sounds like a tap!

One night I was sitting at home in front of a cosy fire, when a music documentary came on BBC4. The programme was called *Don't Stop the Music,* an in-depth profile of the legendary rock band, Fleetwood Mac.

I watched in fascination as the band's tempestuous story unfolded on screen – the arguments, the illicit affairs, the bitter rivalries, the drug taking, the management fallouts (I wasn't the only one then), and all of it taking place while the band wrote these amazing songs, sold millions of albums, and generally conquered the world.

I could only admire their extraordinary drive and creativity, I'd already been a big fan, but now I was a *huge* fan – I was just so inspired and completely taken by their fighting spirit. Go Stevie!

I hadn't planned to watch this documentary; I'd just sort of stumbled upon it by chance. It caught my eye, and I'm glad it had – it was lucky. It's strange how things like that work out. Maybe it was fate, who knows, but if Dad had had *his* way, we'd have been watching the football and I would never have got to see it. Vicky 1, Dad 0.

One of the producers and sound engineers who'd featured strongly in the documentary caught my attention. His name was Ken Caillat, and he'd worked on all the Fleetwood Mac's standout albums – including Rumours and Tusk. He came across as easy-going and approachable, so that's exactly what I did: I approached him.

Soon, after a little Facebook snooping and some messages back and forth, I was off, jet-setting it over the Atlantic to meet the man himself.

Fast Forward; Toothbrush – American Airlines – Sushi in Santa Monica.

Toothbrush because… you should never forget your toothbrush on a long-haul flight; fresh minty breath and dental hygiene should be taken seriously and never overlooked. Healthy teeth and gums – and therefore a gleaming smile – is a must for anyone who talks and sings as much as I do.

American Airlines because… they're reliable, and I like the colour of their planes and the panache of the air stewardess's uniforms.

And Sushi in Santa Monica because… it has the best and freshest seafood on the west coast, caught straight from the Pacific Ocean.

So, after a hectic dash to LAX, there I was, sitting in the breakfast room at the Jamaica Bay Inn Hotel, Marina Del Rey, south east LA – now *that* has a nice ring to it. Kind of poetic, just like my breakfast – fresh pastries and hot chocolate, delicious!

And the view from my table, well, that came straight out of a Bond movie; through a cluster of palm trees, the sun-drenched harbour looked dazzling in the early morning light, a sheaf of tall white sails gently swaying on the Pacific breeze. Bliss.

The marina itself was crammed with vessels big and small, from flashy millionaire's yachts – all gleaming white livery and pristine decks – to macho, twin engine power boats, as aerodynamic as knives and just as deadly, to modest skiffs, bobbing haphazardly at their moorings. The walkways and jetties in front of the hotel were starting to fill up with sun worshipers and would-be captains; their bright bikinis and vivid Bermuda shorts shimmering in the heat like a watercolour painting come to life.

It felt so great to be back in the city of Angels, and I felt like I'd really grown up since my last visit – so much time passed, so many lessons learnt. Despite everything, I was in a really good place and happy and content where I was at.

My younger sister Philippa drank in the view. "It's so freakin' cool here!"

It was her first time in Los Angeles, and she was loving it – the California sun, the pastel-coloured vistas, the cool, laid-back groove, the towering skyscrapers… what's not to like? So far, she'd walked the 'catwalk' on Venice Beach, witnessed its daily carnival of perfect beach bodies flexing and posing, and dodged the eccentric misfits and street entertainers who were always keen for your attention and your dollars! She reminded me of myself, all wide-eyed and innocent, the very first time I'd come to the dream factory six years before.

Finishing the last drops of my green tea, I glanced at my watch: it was time to go to the studio and meet Ken at the famed Village Recorder on Santa Monica Boulevard. It was only a short drive away – just off the 405 San Diego Freeway -- and after leaving the hotel we hopped on the interstate, joining a river of cars bumper-to-bumper heading north.

In less than ten minutes, we were there.

We cruised along the boulevard, turning onto Butler Avenue before stopping outside the studio. Considering its glamorous reputation – not to mention all the famous rock and pop acts that have recorded there – it wasn't much to look at; more like a warehouse if anything, built with red brick and yellow pilasters evenly spaced along the outer walls.

It had a fascinating history, though. Originally a Masonic temple, it had been built by the Freemasons in the 1920's. During the psychedelic 60's, however, it was home to the Los Angeles Centre for Transcendental Meditation, run by Maharishi Mahesh Yogi, a saintly man with a long white beard and flowing robes. Music had long since replaced the contemplative chanting of its devotees, and that was why I was there: to do my chant and sing, rather than ponder the meaning of life. Although who knew? Perhaps I'd do both.

We were first met by the valet parking staff; one of the attendants came rushing over, mildly irate – apparently Dad had parked the car in the wrong direction on the wrong side of the road, which for some reason was a big no-no. Parking etiquette? Aesthetics? I had no idea. But we did as we were told and turned the car around. At least he hadn't driven on the wrong side of the road, like he had done on Melrose one terrifying time before – now Angelinos, that's a proper suicide lane!

Philippa and I entered the studio via a side door situated on

Butler Avenue, a cold blast of air-conditioning washing over us as soon as we were inside. No matter how much I loved the hot LA sunshine, it certainly felt good to escape it for a while. Ken was in reception to meet and greet, meaning lots of hugs and smiles all round. He was the same warm and friendly person I'd encountered in the documentary.

"Well, young lady," he said, a beaming smile on his face. "You're finally here, I'm so glad to meet you Vicky, thanks for coming out here."

"No, thank you Ken, thanks for having me," I replied.

"I really like the songs you sent me. And your voice! As soon as I heard it I just had to meet you… would you like me to show you around?"

Would I! "Yes please," I replied, trying to sound cool.

Actually, it wasn't my first time at the Village – I'd visited a few years before as the owner Jeff Greenberg was a close friend of Tom Ross – but I was eager to see the place again.

Ken gave us a very personal tour, leading us around the atmospheric corridors towards Studio D, the iconic studio where the albums Rumours and Tusk had been recorded by Fleetwood Mac. We passed wall after wall of gold and platinum albums, framed and sandwiched behind polished glass. Reading the names of all the famous artists that had been associated with this studio was dizzying, a real who's who of 20th Century music – The Doors, The Rolling Stones, Eric Clapton, Aerosmith, The Red Hot Chilli Peppers, Pink Floyd, Madonna… the list just went on and on. And OH MY GOD! There was also Karen Carpenter, a voice to die for.

Eventually we reached the top floor and Ken pointed out the various studios. I was like a kid in a sweet shop, eyes on stalks; I just loved it and didn't know what to look at next. In my head, I summoned the ghosts of the past – in my mind's eye I saw Stevie Nicks walking down the corridor, swigging from a bottle of Jack, caught the Chili Peppers flirting with a backing singer, heard the ecstatic guitar licks of Eric Clapton and witnessed Bob Dylan arguing with himself.

If walls could talk!

Finally, we got to Ken's studio – studio E – and inside we met Ghian, Ken's sound engineer. He was a talented guy and very much tuned in to what was happening technically at the mixing desk; he showed me the ins-and-outs of the studio, familiarising me with all the equipment – mics, mixing desks, instruments, drinks machines, you name it! Everything was talked about.

Ken and I went into the control room for a nice chit-chat. We got on well, exchanging musical ideas and generally shooting the breeze. He told me stories about some of the famous people he'd worked with; the parties, the arguments, the creativity. Considering I was an unknown artist, he really went out of his way to make me feel at home. I felt very lucky and grateful. Once the chinwag was over we all decided on lunch and ordered sushi seafood for delivery.

Over the next few days, our friendship grew. He set up a collaboration with one of his writers, Eric Berdon, and we got down to work straight away; writing new songs and working on ideas, one of which was *Human*. I had some lyrics penned and a melody for the chorus, as well as the main theme and vocal path: I wanted it to be a song celebrating being real, flaws and all.

Eric loved the idea, and we completely clicked as we worked on it; the music dust was really flying that day, and the timing couldn't have been more perfect. I wanted to show Ken what I was all about and what I could do and *Human* was a great way to start.

Don't waste time on regret
If you give more than you get
You're gonna be fine, fine, fine
Once you put the past away, you're gonna be OK
Just takes a little time, time, time
When you break through

The ties that try to bind you
Be strong, hold on, let it go…
You'll fly over buildings and skyscrapers
And you'll rise like a force of nature
And you'll run like the wind
Come back where you begin
And you'll find you're more than someone, you're human, human

On Ken's instructions, I slipped into the sound booth, put on a pair of cans, and laid down some backing vocals for a new song I was working on… lots of warm oohs and aahs.

Standing there, at the same music studios Stevie Nicks had graced, I breathed in the musty air, inhaling every last atom and hoping for some musical alchemy to take place. Scanning my surroundings, I soaked in the special moment of singing where so many great singers had sung before. It really was magical, it was the kind of place you felt like John Lennon and Yoko Ono might walk in – its secret doors and passages – its otherworldly spirit and atmosphere. Maharishi Mahesh Yogi once said, *"Life finds its purpose and fulfilment in the expansion of happiness"* – Yes Yogi, I can relate to that, especially here in this place of enlightenment.

Then something just as special happened: KNOCK! KNOCK! The door opened. It was the food delivery guy.

He was here with the sushi!

Glimpses of Me... Put a 100 down and buy a car

Oh crap, this is scarier than I thought!

I was OK driving around in the backstreets of LA, but now the sign for the freeway is coming up! **EAST 101.** *It's going to be my first ever drive on the LA freeway and my heart starts to race as I pull up to stop at the traffic light. It's noisy and dusty – discarded litter blows around in a mad swirl trapped within the concrete walls of the slip road. It's anarchic, and the excitement is starting to kick in.*

A white Dodge pickup pulls up next to me, and the driver casually glances over my way; he's wearing Oakley shades with the windows down and the music on - he's playing it cool – so Cali!

Right, less of that Vicky, concentrate! It's the Los Angeles freeway... get ready, think and focus on the traffic light in front of you...

Red... Green... GO!

Aghhhhhhhh... The Dodge pickup zooms off into the distance, its V8 engine leaving me behind in a cloud of blue dust – hey! he jumped the light! I quickly shift the gear stick into 'drive' and floor the throttle, causing the car to shoot forwards pinning my small frame to the seat. Whoooosh... I'm up the ramp, and I'm gone onto the freeway.

I've been told to drive hard, and not to be timid, oh, and take no prisoners...

Well, here it goes...

12

The final cut

Under leaden skies cloaked in drizzle, the car swung into the inside lane of the M62.

"Keep left," ordered the sat-nav. "Twenty-four miles to your destination."

Ah yes, our destination. Our destination today was Liverpool: the land of the Scousers.

Sitting in the back of the family car, I stared out at the gloomy weather. Ominous grey clouds heavily enshrouded the motorway, the spray from the passing cars streaking the window next to me.

I slumped further into my seat, almost hiding, willing the day to just go away. I was dressed in dull, serious clothes – a suit jacket, plain black trousers, and sensible black boots. Serious clothes for a serious day.

We were driving to Liverpool High Court. The trial with my ex-manager was over, and now it was Judgement Day, a day to be reckoned with.

And I really wasn't looking forward to it.

I'd not slept well the previous night, my mind unable to switch off and wondering what tomorrow would bring. To make matters worse, no matter what I said, my eczema face was back and told part of the story of my sleepless night. I tried to carry on as normal – attempting to trick my brain into thinking that the day was going to be ordinary, just like any other day – but still buried in my subconscious was all the doubt and the fear, the knowing that tomorrow could change everything. *Everything*.

The car sped down the motorway, heading west as it ate up mile after mile of Cheshire countryside. It wasn't the picture-postcard views of Cheshire or the images that were often found in glossy life-style magazines, however; here the terrain had an estuary flatness, providing a kind of monotonous no-man's-land between two great cities.

I watched as a forgotten farmhouse drifted by, its collapsed roof open to the four winds. What dreams the farmer and his family must have had when they'd first moved in. Gone now, of course. His hopes shattered. His disappointment complete. His life possibly over.

Stop it, Vicky!

Suddenly my mobile chirped, interrupting both my bad daydreams and the funeral silence inside the car. I glanced down at the screen. It was my sister, Alexandra.

"Hi, Ally. Yeah, I'm OK… No, we're not there yet… One… We have to be there by one… I'm sure it'll be fine… Yeah, yeah… Got to go now…I'll call you later."

Alexandra is one of the younger sisters, and I could tell by her voice that she was concerned and thinking of me.

Even though my sisters knew what was going on, I still don't think they truly understood the enormity of it all, which was probably a good thing. My parents and I made a conscious effort to keep our family life as normal as possible – even if we were stressed-out at times – especially as we wanted to protect the younger ones.

Of course, even though we tried very hard, it was still extremely difficult to control the raw emotions we were all feeling, especially for my Dad and I, who had been through everything together. There had been many, many heated arguments, tense discussions, door slamming, crying, tears, and breakdowns – you name it, we had done it.

There had also been many times where I'd screamed to get out of the car whilst he was driving and he'd pull over and shout at me to get out. Times where he grabbed anything he could hold, just so he could throw something at me, and times where I pushed him and shouted in a rage in his face. We had moments where we were truly both at breaking point, when our only way of releasing the tension had been to take it out on each other. The tension sometimes felt like a pressure cooker about to explode, and as I sat in the car Liverpool bound, I thought to myself, 'time's up'.

If my ex-manager's aim was to test our father/daughter relationship, well… he had truly succeeded. But by no means had he won, because as much as our relationship was fractious at times, I will always love my Dad, and I know he will always love me.

Love sometimes makes you say and do silly things when you're pushed to the limit, and that we certainly did. It was only because we cared so much. For two years we'd attempted to be brave, hanging on the wire and trying not to look down, as if we were walking a tightrope that could snap at any moment.

Hanging on the wire and I don't look down

Wear a big smile, upside frown

Fear's my friend, I'll fight it to the end

I've got to stand tall, been here before

I know I've gotta be, gotta be, brave, brave, brave

Deep down I was worried. *Really* worried; worried that we might lose the trial, lose our home, and consequently test the very existence of the family. I couldn't believe how things were turning out for me. It's funny in the music business; one-minute people are your best buddies – "You're amazing! You're a star!" – and then next they're throwing you under a bus. Like I've said, it's like playing the board game Snakes and Ladders; when they play, they throw all the sixes, and then when you play, you just end up dodging the snakes.

What really added to my woes though, was being told by my

lawyers that if we *did* lose the trial today, there would likely be another, a new trial on the issue of quantum merit, to determine their losses, they say. What? In plain speak: We'd owe them shedloads of money that we couldn't possibly afford to pay.

The thought of it made me feel queasy, just like how I'd felt in those early singing auditions, my heart in my throat. My stomach empty. Nauseous. Where would we live? How would I tell my sisters? The guilt. It felt too much to comprehend. It wasn't just me who was worried, either. The night before, I'd walked across the hall, overhearing Mum and Dad talking in hushed tones in the kitchen – a snatched conversation full of foreboding.

"What if we...?"

"Lose?"

"Yeah."

"Doesn't bear thinking about, April."

"We'd... We'd have to sell the house, wouldn't we?"

"Probably…"

Pulling off the motorway, we finally entered the outskirts of Liverpool. It looked scruffy, with street after street of Victorian terraces looking dilapidated and gone to the dogs. Groups of kids hung around street corners, eating fast food, while women pushing prams huddled against the rain – no doubt, a once proud part of the city scythed down and disadvantaged by unemployment. Everything I looked at was just wet and miserable. Maybe if it had been sunny I would have been more hopeful, but then again, maybe not. The weather certainly wasn't helping my mood, anyway.

We followed the signs for the Albert Dock, and nearly every passing billboard advertised 'Beatles Cavern Tours' (*The Long and Winding Road – Help – Please Please Me – Let It Be*) Looming over the city were its two magnificent cathedrals, thoughtful presences, each one eyeing the other – the neo-gothic Anglican, the crown-like Roman Catholic.

Eventually we reached the vast car park at the Albert Dock,

where squally gusts of wind lashed at us, as we got out of the car. As the law courts were only a short distance away, Mum suggested we brave the weather and walk – it would do us all good and clear our minds, she said.

As I stretched my legs, a cold breeze caressed my face. I felt tired and lethargic, yet at the same time I wanted to prepare myself for what was to come. I had to wake up and focus, I had to be ready.

As I gazed out across the river Mersey, the late winter sun broke through a bank of cloud, gilding the river in scales of grey and sliver. It looked calm and untroubled. Like many a tourist before me, I couldn't help but sing Gerry and The Pacemakers' famed song, *"Ferry Across the Mersey"* – *'Ferry across the Mersey... da-da-da... da-da-da-da'* – it's impossible not to.

"Let's get this over with," said Dad, resigning himself to the day.

Somewhat reluctantly, we started walking along the waterfront, passing imposing red brick warehouses that shadowed the dock. A century ago this area was full of migrants escaping to the New World – escape! I wish.

Threading a path through this once great seaport, we strolled into the heart of the city. The mood was quiet, the atmosphere damp. Looking up, I watched the hands of the four-sided clock on the Liver Building tick round to o'clock.

Tick-tock.

Tick-tock.

Back in the Queen Elizabeth II Law Courts. We went through the usual checks – bags, coats, shoes – a wave of the security wand beckoning us in. A familiar face was there to greet us; our trusted lawyer, Brian. By now Brian was almost part of the family, we'd spent so much time with him. He'd become like a distant relative that you were forced to meet up with at family occasions, and then had grown to like.

"How are you all feeling?" he asked.

"We're fine, just wet."

"Well, not to worry, the hearing's about to begin. Follow me."

He hurried us into the courtroom, the sight of the royal crest above the judge's dais making quite the statement. It was a different court this time, but with some of the same familiar faces, not to mention that smell again; a reek of polished wood and musty garb. Ah, the scent of the judiciary!

"All rise!"

Doing as we were told we got to our feet, my heart fluttering, a trapped bird in a cage. The time has come.

A side door opened and Judge Hodge entered the court, a resplendent figure robed in wig and gown. He was carrying a thick bundle of papers; the judgement, according to Brian. Considering the size of it, this would take some time to read. I didn't relish the thought. I could feel my eyes start to glaze over.

The judge nodded and took his seat, then the Clerk of the Court stood up.

Clearing his throat, he announced in a firm voice, "Today's hearing is between the parties Arkace and Leobright Limited – the claimants – and Vicky Nolan – the defendant."

There was a respectful murmur around the room. The court was now in session.

"Quiet please! Judge Hodge will now read his judgement."

As the judge began to read, I stole a quick glance to my left, towards the benches where my ex-manager and his legal counsel would be sitting. I wanted to see his face, I wanted to see his reaction as the judgement was read out.

He wasn't there.

I stared up at the glass skylight in the ceiling of the courtroom, the pitter patter noise of the rain attracting my attention – it sounded strangely comforting, reminding me of my early childhood at school, when the rain used to fall against the classroom windows.

The judge addressed the court, peered over his wired spectacles, then looked up and began to speak. His monotone voice spoke at the same slow pace, he talked and talked without pause, only occasionally stopping for small sips of water whilst turning the pages of his judgement. I looked at my watch, thinking this could be a long day.

Soon his voice began to rise and fall in soft tones… sounding like the gentle showers of the rain falling against the glass on the skylight above, the soft sprinkle of rain, backwards and forwards, it was comfortably hypnotic, him softly talking and the sound of the sprinkling of the rain, softer and softer, making me feel tired and sleepy… drowsy and sleepy... drifting… slipping to sleep…. drifting… the sound of the rain, pitter patter… pitter patter… pitter patter… drifting… slipping… falling… falling down a hole… falling to sleep… dreaming, dreaming… pit… pat… tick… tick…

…tick… tick… watching the metronome on top of the piano swaying in time… tick… tick… tick… tick… the metronome beats in time… tick… tick… tick…tick…

What was that?… Sing, Vicky?… Sing?… Why?… Because I am your music teacher and you were born to sing, dear… Where am I?… You're back in Mrs Nield's music room, dear. The sheet music blows and swirls around madly, and the windows are loudly rattling wide open, but she never leaves the windows open… the cats will escape! Am I going mad! "Oh, you can't help that," said the cat: "We're all mad here". Oh no, the cat's talking! cats! All those smiling cats! Cat hair! Cat hair everywhere! I can't breathe, Mrs Nield, please, I can't breathe! I'm trying to do my scales but I can't breathe!

"Concentrate, Vicky. Concentrate. Your scales are almost done now, but don't forget, the competition's in two weeks. You must be ready for it, now carry on listening to the metronome…"

"Yes, Mrs Nield…. Do Re Mi Fa…"

"Watch the metronome, Vicky."

"Yes, Mrs Nield, I will…"

Tick… tick… tick… tick… The metronome beats in time. Tick… tick… tick… tick…

The audience swoon, the stage lights dazzle…. Applause, applause…. Oh no, I'm still falling and I can't stop falling…. Applause, applause…. Take a bow… take a bow. Backstage I read Mrs Nields note, tucked into a spray of flowers…

'*A bouquet for the star on her opening night. Let your voice soar and the audience will soar with yo*u,' but they won't because you've **gone!!**

I can see what's bothering me

Oh, she can see, she wants to make you believe

You've got a ghost living on your street

It's spooking out the neighbours

You've got a ghost living in your heart

You've got a ghost I'd like to meet

So I don't feel a stranger.

Tick… tick… tick… tick… The metronome beats in time. Tick… tick… tick… tick…

Look, Mrs Nield! I'm soaring over Los Angeles! I'm floating down Melrose Avenue and it's sooooooo cool! The gardens. The heat. The glamour. Look at me, I'm all grown up and I'm in an American car; I can drive. I can actually drive! What? Why? Why is it doing that? The car won't stop. The brakes won't work. I can't stop! They won't work, quick Mrs Neild, my brakes won't work and I'm running out of road, I'm going to crash! Make it stop! PLEASE!!

"Why it's simply impassible!" says Mrs Neild.

"Why, don't you mean impossible?"

"*No,* I mean impassable… now listen to the metronome Vicky, or you'll crash."

Tick… tick… tick… tick… The metronome beats in time. Tick… tick… tick… tick…

All around me is blue glass, dazzling blue glass… a cheesy grin, welcome to our Pacific Design Centre, Miss, welcome to our blue whale, please just follow the corridor down to the room at the end… Turning the door handle, I close my eyes and step in… oh NO! It's empty! It's an empty white room with no windows and now no door… where's the door gone? How do I get out?!

"Would you like some wine?"

"Where did you appear from?"

"DRINK ME"

"No!"

"Name please."

"Vicky Nolan."

"Sorry, your name's not on the list."

"It IS on the list."

"Who told you that?"

"EVERYONE!!!!"

"There's only one person who can let you out, and he's on the other side of that door. Go on. He's waiting for you… he's waiting to tell you something."

I make a frantic grab for the door handle and rush through the doorway, then there's just a moment of calm. It's quiet, blurry and quiet, slowly my eyes begin to blink open…

Pitter patter rain, pitter patter … pit… pat… pit…pat…. pit…. pat…… stop.

I'm awake, back in the room and out of my head. I'm back here looking at the glass skylight in the courtroom, the rain's stopped now, the clouds are going away, and the sun is coming out. Yes, I'm awake, I'm back in the court, back in front of the judge... Here, and there's nowhere to hide and no dream to escape back into…

Judge Hodge was still speaking, the clarity of his voice now waking me up fully as he came to the end of his reading, making his points on the relevant law. It was still all gobbledegook to me, but as he was drawing to his conclusion, I leaned forward, ready to pay him 100% of my attention.

Turning the final page of his trial notes, he looked out towards my ex-manager's bench and legal team. After raising his head, he came to his judgement: " So, In the case of Arkace and Leobright Limited verses Vicky Nolan, I find for…"

A new sun rising in the east

A new dawn calling out to me

I leave the shadows far behind

'cause now I'm feeling unstoppable

I don't need an umbrella

Cause I'm feeling better

I tell you I'm moving on, 'cause those days are gone

The rain clouds are gone and I'm moving on and I'm moving up

Glimpses of Me... Writers Block

"Let me show you this hilarious video of a dog skateboarding…"

"Oh, and I've got to show you this amazing girl who tap dances whilst singing with a vintage band…"

"Have you heard of Lennon and Maisy from Nashville? You should cover their song Telescope…"

Every session with Ellie and Phillipa starts with a cup of tea, a catch up and all of us sharing our favourite things that we have found from the internet. We put the world's wrongs to right, we talk about life, our feelings, dreams, fears, things that make us laugh and make us cry. There's no topic off limits. It's essentially therapy with harmonies.

We sometimes draw inspiration from strange places.

"I love the sound of music that's played for 5 seconds at the end of this Sex in the City episode… Let's recreate it!"

"Ok, so we're pitching for a kitsch, Japanese pop band. It needs to be about fun and all about girl power… I've got a theme idea to start: Bubblegum. What do you think?!"

Sometimes we get writers block and have to crack open the biscuits whilst we reboot. But most of the time we write about love, life and everything that we hope to be someday.

INT CAR - DAYTIME - MANCHESTER - RAINING

VICKY (aged 13) and MUM are pulling up in
the car outside the music school - VICKYS
sisters are sat in the back of the car.

                    MUM

Right Vicky, I'll be back in an hour, when
                   you've

            finished your exam.

                   VICKY

  But, but mum... what if I finish early?

                    MUM

You won't finish early, they said an hour,
                    and

          I'll be back before...

SISTERS start being noisy from the back of
the car. MUM turns around.

                    MUM

    Quiet!... you'll wake Elizabeth.

                   VICKY

    Can I do it another day Mum?

                    MUM

Don't be silly Vicky! Your music exam is
               booked in

                    160

for today, the adjudicators are waiting
for you now!

Now don't worry, I know your nervous, but
you'll be

fine. Honest!

VICKY frowns and looks towards the
entrance door at the school.

                    MUM

        Go on...you'll be OK

VICKY collects her music bag and opens the
car door, then leans forward and kisses
her MUM on her cheek.

                    VICKY

        Love you Mum!

13

Call the publisher

A chill December wind blew down the village high street as Park Lane, Poynton prepared for Christmas. Workmen were busy on ladders putting up the Christmas street lights and decorations, shopkeepers were doing their bit too, displaying fairy lights and festive garlands in their shop windows to cheer up the cold winter days. After all, it was the season of goodwill!

Wrapped up warmly in a bobble hat and scarf, Mum slowly made her way along the lane towards the post office. She was pushing baby Lizzy in her baby buggy, making sure to tread carefully over the frost-covered pavement.

Directly across the road was the spire of our local church, St. George's, pointing its icy finger towards Heaven – it was the place where Mum and Dad had got married and where we were all christened.

Finally reaching the post office, Mum squeezed the buggy through the door and made her way to the shop counter. Baby Lizzy started to sniffle and cry, her hat had slipped down covering her eyes and face, this was Mum's cue for a cuddle.

As the bells from St. Georges chimed, she noticed the early edition of the Manchester Evening News newspaper on the newsstand. This was what she had walked into the village for. With a sense of expectation, she went over to pick up a copy of the newspaper, and as the bold banner headline jumped into sharp focus, she read…

I'M FREE!... judge ends 24-YEAR deal with manager

Nodding in quiet agreement, Mum smiled. She already knew this, of course, but she wanted to read it for herself in black-and-white, she wanted to know it was for real, it was true, and it was over. Finally.

She read on:

'...after a row with her manager, Vicky has won a legal case...'

Baby Elizabeth starts to wave her arms around, making a grab for the newspaper – mum undeterred, kept reading.

'...armed with a bottle of champagne. He signed the teenager to a management contract with his company, Arkace Ltd, and to another deal with his second company, Leobright Ltd, which gave him rights over any recordings she might go on to release...'

We never did drink the champagne, she thought.

'...Judge Hodge praised the teenager as a "confident, relaxed, assured, intelligent and engaging individual" whose evidence was both reliable and truthful...'

Mum took it all in, feeling a deep sense of emotion "I'm so proud of you Vicky," she whispered, before baby Lizzy finally made her last successful grab for the newspaper, finally making her point as she seized it and tore into it, crumpling the paper and tearing the newsprint apart.

Mum smiled down at her. "You're right, Lizzy – it's finished with, time for Peppa Pig. I've read enough. It's time to go home."

If it's hard then you will know it's meant to be
It will come eventually
Doors may close
But take the opportunity
Life is full of possibility

LAW FIRM OFFICE - NORTH HOLLYWOOD - DAYTIME - HOT - FREEWAY TRAFFIC NEARBY

JAY - Vicky's Attorney picks up the phone looks up at the ceiling fan, wipes his brow and makes a call to VICKY.

Fade in :

Pause the phone rings.

INT VICKY'S BEDROOM - DAYTIME - CHESHIRE - SUNNY

VICKY'S waiting for a call from her attorney in North Hollywood, her iPhone rings on the bed. She reaches down and answers

                    VICKY
                 Hello...

                    JACOB
                Hey Vicky,...

                    VICKY
        Hi Jacob, how you doing, any news?

JACOB

(PAUSES)

Yes, it's not looking good... their
position hasn't

changed really, the film production
company still wants to own all of the
copyrights to the music in perpetuity.
Virtually forever Vic. I can't recommend
it.

VICKY

Arrghh, that's not good... and we've come
such a long Way with this deal.

JACOB

I know! I've said it before... these
people have got Shark

Records written all over them... It's time
to walk

away Vicky.

Fade out:

14

Sorry... Was I out of Key?

A smartly dressed waiter escorted me to my table, he sat me down close to an open fire, its fierce heat toasting my back – strange, they had a fire lit on such a fine London day. Outside through a set of patio doors, I could see the early afternoon sun glinting off a bank of skyscrapers surrounding the rooftop pool. We were sitting on the top floor of a private member's club - Shoreditch House, in the East End – an uber-cool establishment frequented by artists, musicians, and the media elite. Based in a converted warehouse overlooking the City's square mile, it's the same club where Madonna and Jennifer Aniston have celebrated their birthdays. It's more East Side New York than East End London. I love the place! My boyfriend Ed was a member and has got me a reservation for the afternoon.

I was there to have lunch with top music executive Bryant Reid - CEO of B Street Entertainment. Hailing from Atlanta Georgia, Bryant was a well-established music exec with an amazing track record - a snappy dresser who turned heads wherever he went. He found and signed the R&B artist Usher to his brother's record label, LaFace – he'd also worked closely with Toni Braxton (whom I love!)

I could see him coming towards me through the crowded club, he wasn't hard to miss, immaculately groomed as usual – he was wearing a pale blue jacket, crisp linen trousers, white shirt, candy striped tie and a jaunty panama. I was looking for a manager and hoped he was the one. I'd sent him some demos a few months before and he'd asked me to arrange a showcase case gig for when he next came over to London; somewhere trendy where he could see me shine. I had been asked to perform at a well-established music night in Notting Hill and thought it was the perfect opportunity for him to see me sing. It wasn't exactly what he had asked for but it was the best I could do on my non-existent budget. Then, hours before I was set to perform, he had to cancel his trip due to family illness in the States. I was disappointed because it turned out to be a brilliant showcase. The crowd loved my set and I sang with a fabulous acoustic guitarist. I had also managed to get lots of support from about 20 family and friends who came along specially to whoop and cheer giving the impression that I was more popular than I was.

A few weeks later Bryant asked me to arrange a second showcase, which was a real challenge second time round. I told him I needed some help finding the right venue; help putting a band together and a plan so I could fund it all. I felt completely out of my depth. That's what I thought our lunch date was all about, a joint powwow to put a plan together. How naive was I?

Greeting me, with a warm Southern smile, we embraced and welcomed one another with the customary kisses to both cheeks. We took our seats and sat down. He told me he was staying at the Mandeville Hotel not far from the US Embassy in Grosvenor Square - very luxurious! He ordered a round of drinks from the waiter and then we looked at the menus. I asked him if he'd come up with any ideas for my upcoming showcase.

Suddenly his body language changed. His sunny smile faded, replaced by a world-weary look. He shook his head woefully. "I have to say Vicky I'm very disappointed. I asked you to arrange a simple thing like a showcase and you didn't deliver. I expected more from you."

My heart sunk into my shoes. I had let him down and I felt awful... I had misread him completely. Just weeks before I had put together a successful showcase that due to unfortunate circumstances he couldn't attend, and now this. My attempt at recreating the magic the second time round had failed. I should have never got him to see me perform in a noisy, dingy sports bar in Covent Garden, I felt stupid. The star quality he had wanted to witness, obviously didn't shine through.

"Come on, Vicky, you and I both know it's not just about the gig. You're a talented girl, amazingly so, otherwise I wouldn't have flown across the Atlantic to be here. You didn't deliver what I wanted." He pointed through the patio doors of the club, waving his Rolex encrusted hand towards the City of London. "Do you know how many kids there are out there who'd give anything to be in your shoes right now? Do you? Millions. Let me tell you something. I've got huge plans for you in the States. There's a recording deal and a TV show in the pipeline. It's all there if you want it, but you have to show me some desire."

Stunned, I sat there in silence. I didn't know what to say. It was true. I looked upon Bryant as a mentor, so to be told that I had disappointed him especially in such a kind and gentlemanly way, knocked me for six.

I spent many minutes explaining and apologising but deep down I knew he was right. It always seemed that when I got my opportunity to make it across the finish line I always stalled. I dragged my feet. Did I really want this life? Do I really want to be a recording artist? Or was I just scared? I got to my feet slowly. "Please excuse me, I'm just going to the ladies."

I put cold water on my neck to cool me down from the intense conversation and roaring fire. I took a few deep breaths and took a long hard look at myself in the mirror, analysing everything Bryant had said to me. To be honest, I wasn't too sure about aiming for America again. As much as I loved the land of opportunity, and its amazing positivity, deep down, I adored my life as it was - in London.

At this time, I was starting to feel happy with my life and the choices I was making. I was about to move to Bethnal Green in London and live and setup home with my boyfriend Ed - much to the disagreement of my parents. I was in a lovely relationship and he was incredibly supportive. I also knew that the possibility of success in the States would mean a tremendous amount of time and dedication, away from London, and home.

Could I give it my all? Could I achieve this with an empty bank account, no plan and no manager? I wasn't sure I was cut out for it. I'd often read about how many of my favourite artists had lived on nothing and managed to make it big through sheer determination and talent. I'm not sure if I could do it; I was already finding it incredibly testing. That was the missing ingredient, money. SHOW ME THE MONEY! Not money for designer clothes or luxury hotels, but money to drive my project forward and make the vision a reality. Problem was, everyone I met seemed to talk the talk but not walk the walk. No action, just promises. Same old chit chat. I was travelling back and forth to London to be with Ed, juggling jobs so I could gig weekly at open-mic nights around the capital. I was working with photographers and producers, networking on Myspace, pulling favours, attending auditions, singing at a small ASCAP workshop where Ed Sheeran also performed, lunching with Jessie J who was friends with my song writing partner, getting backstage passes to Ronnie Scott's and mingling with industry folk. I had finally learnt how to blag! I hung around in all the right circles but always seemed to miss out on that lucky break. Because let's face it, no matter how talented you are, luck is everything – being in the right place at the right time, meeting the right people. It got me thinking that maybe the fates were against me, or maybe it just wasn't my time.

Speaking of time; It seemed I spent much of it worrying if I'd ever be good enough to succeed – this at times, making me sometimes slightly depressed. I felt really down about the pressure and constraints heaped upon me from a young age (my friends were all at University – living it up and having a ball) I'm not blaming anyone for this, after all I went into the music scene with my eyes open, but eventually the knock backs and high expectations take its toll. For someone who's pretty 'together' and thrives on routine, the lack of any clear plan for the future made me feel terribly lost. Mum and Dad were different from most parents in the way that they encouraged me *not* to work or study (yes, you read that right), and instead focus on my art, pushing me to network my ass off. I found this very difficult to do 100% of the time.

So, at that very moment, in the posh lady's loo at Shoreditch House, I decided on a different approach. I would train my brain and develop a more positive attitude. I knew if I wanted to be happy then I had to move to London full time - to spread my wings and become independent even if my parents didn't think it was the right decision. They were incredibly protective and always had my best interests at heart but sometimes, in the words of Fleetwood Mac, you have to *'Go Your Own Way'*. I had to focus on living, go off-course and enjoy life, and write and sing about it (material for my art). Then, hopefully, my time would come.

Glimpses of Me... Bollywood Nights

Am I really here? Standing on this beautiful Mauritian beach? Working as a butler, holding a tray of Pepperoni pizza like a schmuck?! And it's not even for me! Nope, I'm not imagining it, I'm here... I can feel the sugary sand between my toes, and yes, if I'm not mistaken that's the sound of the ocean lapping at my feet — and I can definitely feel the cool evening air caressing my pink sun-burnt skin.

The sky is streaked purple, red and gold, the vast Indian Ocean spread out before me on this curving bay of white sand. I'm in paradise, holding pizza! When I signed up for this job I didn't quite imagine I'd be feeding a bride lemonade through a straw and holding her purse whilst she danced. It definitely was different!

In the centre of this beach party, surrounded by party guests, is the wedding bride Shetal, dancing hypnotically to an Indian Bhangra beat, she looks captivating in her teal blue sari, gyrating to the music that she's lost in. Cobra moves and pulsating hips holds her audience in a trance - Henna painted hands, jewelled encrusted nails, trinkets and gold lockets — she's the epitome of the perfect Indian bride.

The music suddenly stops, on a loud drum beat.... then a moment of silence... then the loud clap of fireworks flaring into the blackened sky. Everyone holler's and cheers.... I'm part of this incredible Bollywood scene.

Shetal signals to me and waves me over towards her.... "Vickee!......... Vickee!........ Come quickly now! I'm hungry, where's my pizza?"

15

A public performance

"Play, music! And you, brides and bridegrooms all, With measure heap'd in joy, to the measures fall.
– William Shakespeare

I drove past the wrought iron gates, turned left, then raced up the leafy road, lined with beautiful lime and oak trees. Suddenly I felt like I was in a Gainsborough painting – one of those timeless English landscapes of undulating parkland, dotted with trees and ornamental follies.

Slowing down, a horse-drawn carriage decorated in lilac flowers, silk ribbons and paper red hearts clip-clopped by my car, the gallant coachman perched on the back kindly tipping his hat towards me as he passed. I quickly wound down my window and called back to him, stopping him and the carriage in its tracks.

"How far to the house?" I shouted.

"Yes, this is the start… and go on till you come to the end: then stop." He replied.

"Thank you," I mouthed curiously.

The scene was enchanting, so enchanting that I wouldn't have been surprised if Mr Darcy rode by on a horse, took off his top, jumped in the lake and went for a swim. Driving carefully on up the uneven road, I crested the brow of the hill where I could just about see the house up ahead looming into view; its blue slate roof and top floor windows glinting in the sun. Wow, this place was big, I thought – *really* big – it was like the house in TV's *Downton Abbey*. It was the kind of place you'd dream of buying with a huge Lottery win. Yes, Lady Mary, if I were to only have such good luck!

The road curved to the right before opening out onto a sweeping gravel drive, which was dominated by a large, elegant fountain. Taking a breath, I pulled up in front of the house, finally having arrived at my destination: Botleys Mansion, Surrey. A Georgian pile of a house made of honey-coloured stone and built in the Palladian style. The mansion had row after row of large sash windows, all with little square windowpanes of glass – a window cleaner's nightmare, I'd imagine.

A sweeping stone staircase led up to the imposing entrance doors – I sat there for a second, just looking up and staring at the grandeur of it all, my imagination bubbling away. I thought about all the swanky parties the aristos must have held here years ago – the house ablaze with light, vintage Rolls Royce cars pulling up, the dapper gents stepping out of their vehicles and escorting their ladies, all glittering in their flapper dresses as they alighted their carriages. Splendidly Majestic!

And there was I, a poor dressed-down troubadour in my old beaten-up Volkswagen Golf! It didn't really have *quite* the same effect.

A smartly-dressed man suddenly appeared at the front door, he gave my car the once over and then came rushing down the stone staircase. He was walking quickly, crunching across the gravel towards me as though I'd done something wrong – perhaps I'd gone the wrong way? Perhaps I wasn't supposed to park there? Perhaps, perhaps…

Getting out of the car, I stood there on the drive, trying to look at home in this grand setting as the man came towards me.

"Name?" he asked, rather snootily.

"Hello," "I'm Vicky Nolan. I'm meeting Andrea Daresbury and Charlie Dodgson in the Green Room.

After producing a black leather folder and opening it up, his eyes started scanning a list clipped to the inside (these people always have lists, don't they?), then – finally – his expression softened as he came across my name. "Oh yes, Vicky. Please follow me, come this way, do you have any luggage?" I told him yes, but insisted that I could carry it myself – but he wouldn't hear of it – and was kind enough to help me carry it out of my car. So we huffed and puffed with the luggage and heavy boxes up to the top of the stairs, and then finally we managed to put everything down in the reception hall.

"Please, do take a seat," he said, out-of-breath, as he pointed to a gilded throne chair. I nodded obligingly, plonking my little bum onto the satin seat. I was glad of the rest, and not just from dragging the boxes in – it had been a long car journey.

As I sat there I took in my surroundings, looking around in awe; it was as if I'd been transported back to Ancient Greece! The room was a symphony in marble – black and white tiled floor, high stuccoed ceiling sprouting a twinkling crystal chandelier, and pristine white walls decorated with swags and medallions.

The hushed atmosphere was very much like that of a temple, and I was aware of every movement I made, as well as every sound, no matter how small. Ionic marble columns – flecked with tiny veins of pink – stood either side of a jet black grand piano, its dark surface polished and shining like a mirror; it was clearly the star attraction of the room.

To add to the scene, a trio of supreme classical statues – Diana, Aphrodite, and Venus - *Ross, Wilson, and Ballard* – stared out from deep niche recesses within the wall, while the rest of the room was completely flooded with white light from the large sash windows at the front. It was a Joy (Floy Joy!).

I sighed, and took a look at myself, sitting there in my Zara off-the shoulder midi dress and strappy high heels surrounded by my big ugly black boxes, the modern looking so juxtaposed, and out of place in these ornate surroundings. I looked a bit like a still life contemporary art installation.

Just for something to do, I grabbed a bottle of water from my bag and took a quick swig. Every few moments a door opened, and I'd watch as a member of staff walked across the reception hall, smiling at me curiously.

Before long, a trickle of guests began to arrive – men in smart suits, women in posh frocks, and well-groomed children with shiny faces and neatly combed hair – and soon the reception hall was full, packed with people shaking hands and embracing one another (some rather tearfully), their chattering voices mixed in laughter and joy. People were having fun; it was a joyful day.

Smiling, I sat back, feeling at one with the gayety of the occasion, and after taking another sip of water I began to softly sing to myself, humming gentle notes and sweet melodies to a tune, remembering and emphasising the words of the song, remembering back to a past time, whispering the lyrics under my breath… "So much of life ahead… So much of life ahead…"

Then, through the crowd of guests, a young girl caught my eye; fair in complexion, about nine years old, she was skipping around in a dainty pair of black shoes, wearing a pale blue dress, giggling and laughing, inquisitive in nature. Her long blonde hair was held up with a hair band and teased into a mass of curls, framing her blue-eyed face, she was clearly the centre of attention – you could tell that by the way each guest reacted to her as she flustered by, she had a wonderful persona. There was something about her sweet personality that chimed with me – like me, at about that age, she found herself at the centre of attention.

As I watched her, she zoned in on me and came running over, full of curious confidence.

"Hello," she said.

"Hello," I replied, smiling and leaning forward.

"What's your name?" she asked, "Are you a singer?"

"My names Vicky." I smiled again. "Yes I am."

Her eyes widened.

"My name's Alicia… I want to be a singer!" she said beaming, whilst doing a little dance.

"You do? That's great" I replied. "It's what I wanted to be when I was your age, and now I am." I shrugged, as though it was no big deal. A piece of cake. Easy-peasy!

Then, she peered up, and gazed into my eyes, her little face changing expression, blanking over, her thought's seemingly taken to a different place, she was in a trance. Perhaps, then imagining herself as a pop star, singing and performing on a stage to a big audience – a seminal moment – maybe this was a mini sliding door moment for cute Alicia? – Which road do I take? Who knows!

When I was little, I'd dreamt that one day I might be a singer. I remember having that sense of wonderment, that feeling of being completely mesmerised, and that feeling immediately owned me. I couldn't shake it and that feeling never went away.

My music teacher, Mrs Nield, told me that if I wanted, I could be a singer one day, and while the thought had elated me then, I think it still does now. Of course, it seemed a bit silly at the time to dare dream such a fanciful thing… Me… Really? Who in the world am I? Maybe it's important for everyone to have a dream.

Year by year, I edged closer and closer to making my pop star fantasy a reality, but daring to dream scared me – as with anything big or intimidating in life, I was frightened at the prospect of putting myself out there.

I used to get painfully shy, and sometimes I would end up holding myself back (perhaps on purpose) when on stage or in meetings with influential people. At the age of 16 I was still so young, like a baby calf falling over its own legs. I knew I was mature for my age, but I just hadn't found *me* yet. Maybe you never truly find yourself? I think we're all on a path to self-discovery and all of the ups and downs are just part of the journey. I would often look out of my window, feeling caged in by my four-bedroom walls, wondering if I'd ever be able to overcome my self-doubt and fears… wondering if I'd ever have what it takes to make it. Not just with my music, but in life.

Perhaps I should have enrolled into a sort of 'Fame Academy School', to help me nurture my talents and further my ambition…

but for me, I was always too independent, out on my own, doing it for myself. As hard as it was I couldn't imagine doing it any other way.

Looking back and wondering why I acted so shy, oh well.

Playing over that scene in my mind, wish I could rewind, then again.

This flashback got me thinking of some of my own sliding door moments. I once wrote a song *("Sing My Song" VNolan/JGosling/CLeonard)* about breaking up with my high school sweetheart and having no regrets. When I shared the song on MySpace, an A&R scout at Warners heard it, and liked it. Two months later he was my boyfriend, and he still is.

I've always wondered about that. I mean, if I hadn't written that song, would we have still met? If the song had turned out differently, would he still have got in touch? What if he'd heard it, disliked it, and had simply moved onto the next person? That's the thing about sliding door moments, we have them every day and don't even realise it.

It could have been different, that's how it goes, but I'm OK,

And I wouldn't change how I've stumbled on my way.

I'm living my life as consequence of yesterday,

And all of my choices complement my life today.

There may have been times I could have gone and lost my way,

I could have, I would have, I should have, I don't care – I'm here now.

One of my favourite writer's, Paulo Coelho said, "You are what you believe yourself to be" and it's this belief that is something we continually learn and grow from. It's the possibility of having a dream that makes life interesting.

So far, I'm just enjoying the ride and embracing the life experiences it brings me – the good and the bad! I've embraced the good, because well, that's a no-brainer really… but maybe weirdly, I've learnt to embrace the bad too. All of our life experiences make us who we are, they shape us into the people we become, and so If it wasn't for the bad, I'd be somebody else.

So, for me, there are no regrets, no sense in looking back, only forwards with an honest spirit – saying that, I did go back once… for my favourite cheese burger and fries at Carneys in Studio City, LA… and guess what? It didn't taste the same.

It's funny how we strive to take control but situations take hold of you.
We try to break free, escape the mould, but life is untold.
It could have been different, that's how it goes, but I'm OK,
I wouldn't change how I've stumbled on my way.

Just like that! the little girl shrugged her shoulders, and snapped out of her daydream. "Goodbye," she said smartly, turned around, and like a gust of wind, she was gone, back into the crowd of guests - playing and dancing – probably back to her own reality.

I too was living in my reality.

My biggest ever confession was the one I gave myself: I didn't want to chase the Pop Star dream anymore. Que Sera, Sera… whatever will be, will be.

But isn't this what you've been striving for? I'd often asked myself. What you've been working so hard for all your life? Yes, I'd replied, but I'm also *so much more* than that.

Once I'd admitted this to myself, all of my fears evaporated in an instant. I became unshackled from the chains that had been making me silently unhappy for all of these years and I felt finally free to enjoy the music again.

Just like all of my fellow collaborators and the music people I know, we're all involved for the love of it, for the joy of making the music, and for the lifelong friendships we make. I suppose, we measure our success by the happiness and contentment we exist in, and when the destination is good music, well… you know it's the real thing.

I'm living life and it's right that I'm here now,

Can't you tell by the way I appear now?

I could have, I would have, I should have, I don't care – I'm here now.

As if pulled from a daydream, I drifted back into the room. I could hear the sound of voices and footsteps approaching me, echoing throughout the large marble hall. Looking up, I saw little Alicia walking towards me, holding hands with a middle-aged lady, all dressed up for the occasion wearing a big fancy regal hat – maybe the grooms mother?

"Hello," said the lady, gleefully. "Are you Vicky? I've been asked to come and fetch you. Alicia has been talking all about you"

Alicia gave me a sweet, grown-up grin.

"Oh yes!" I said, sitting up and trying to look awake and professional.

"Everyone is being seated, follow me"

From the reception hall, I was led down a series of corridors, the walls of which were lined with seemingly endless pictures and portraits – distinguished-looking men on horseback, flighty teenage girls dressed in clouds of taffeta and lace, and haughty duchesses in billowing ball gowns – all lovingly painted in rich oils. One by one they stared down at me as I walked past, each one from a bygone age and yet each one somehow seeming familiar and relevant. We turned left, passing the kitchens, giving me a brief glimpse of steaming copper pans and a whir of the cook's whites. I breathed in the peppered aroma of cooking as I heard the clinking sound of cutlery. Then, finally, we approached the Green Room.

I was just about to go in when little Alicia tugged on my sleeve, glancing up at me excitedly and saying, "Good luck, Vicky!" Such kindness!

The lady opened the white palatial doors, and a moment later I was greeted with rows and rows of guests, seated on chairs that were garlanded with beautiful white roses. Everyone was in place, and everything was perfect, the room bright in the dazzling sun, its rays bouncing off the gold candle chandelier hanging in the centre of the room and sending sparkles of light onto the mint green walls and white plaster friezes.

Quietly, I walked across the oak planked floor towards the corner of the room where I was reunited with my black speaker boxes, positioned on the small stage. I was trying to be inconspicuous, but I knew I wasn't – it was far too quiet for that, and I could feel everyone's eyes on me as I quietly powered-up my PA system and adjusted the mic stand.

Well, this was it. I'm here now.

I preened my hair, reapplied some lipstick, and then looked out at the audience, addressing their friendly faces.

Then, the glowing bride and her handsome groom entered the room and took to the dance floor. Everybody hushed.

"Hello and good afternoon, everyone," I announced. "My name is Vicky Nolan. I'm your wedding singer for this special day. I'd like to perform a song from a favourite singer of mine, for a very special couple."

The bride and groom looked at one another and lovingly embraced. I gestured them a smile, and then pressed the 'play' button on the PA console.

Stepping forward onto the stage, I held the mic, looked up, and waited for the music. The room fell silent.

Chords G major, D, and B… Melody A, C, and E…

I smiled once more, then sang.

"We've only just begun…"

The Outro

To everyone mentioned in the book, my family, friends and fellow musical collaborators, thank you for being part of my journey and scrapbook experience.

To all of the dreamers, this book is dedicated to you.

Vicky x